# J O U R N A L S

Booze 30
Records/watch 50
food 20
ticket 100
―――――――――
200
100

# KURT

# COBAIN

# JOURNALS

RIVERHEAD BOOKS

NEW YORK

Most Riverhead Books are available at special quantity discounts for bulk purchases
for sales promotions, premiums, fund-raising, or educational use.
Special books, or book excerpts, can also be created to fit specific needs.

For details, write: Special Markets, The Berkley Publishing Group,
375 Hudson Street, New York, New York 10014.

RIVERHEAD BOOKS
Published by The Berkley Publishing Group
A division of Penguin Group (USA) Inc.
375 Hudson Street
New York, New York 10014

Notebook covers appearing on front of printed case and
pages 11, 159, and 215: Notebook Cover Design Copyright © 1985,
The Mead Corporation. Used with permission. The image of *The Thanksgiving Scroll*
(Qumran, Roman period, 1st century CE) on page 262 appears courtesy of
The Shrine of the Book, The Israel Museum, Jerusalem.
Photo © The Israel Museum.

Copyright © 2002, 2003 by The End of Music, LLC
Art direction, cover design, and book design by Claire Vaccaro
Digital photography by Nick Vaccaro

First Riverhead hardcover edition: November 2002
First Riverhead trade paperback edition: November 2003
Riverhead trade paperback ISBN: 1-57322-359-X

The Library of Congress has catalogued the Riverhead hardcover edition as follows:
Cobain, Kurt, 1967-1994.
Journals / Kurt Cobain.
p.   cm.
ISBN 1-57322-232-1
1. Cobain, Kurt, 1967-1994—Diaries.
2. Rock musicians—United States—Diaries.
ML420.C59 A3      2002                    2002031690
782.42166'092—dc21
[B]

Printed in the United States of America

3   5   7   9   10   8   6   4   2

Don't read my diary when I'm gone

OK, I'm going to work now, when you
wake up this morning, please read my
diary. Look through my things,
and figure me out.

# JOURNALS

**Dale,** count howmany times i use the word "FUCK".

# Hello, it is me saying

"everything is basically raining, dull, and ok." fuck we were this close ————➔ to coming down to see the melvins play on the 29th but as history repeats itself, shelli being the overbearing dominator of chris decided to not want to go at the last minute. and so gas money being split only two ways between tracy and I would be too fucking expensive. are you coming to seattle someday to play? YOU MOTHERFUCKERS BETTER STILL PLAY VILE VERMILLION VACANCY! or at least put it on the next LP. any label interest yet? Alchemy seems to be in pretty sorry shape from what i hear. ever rat sub core Dave Portnow? Dehumanizers? the reason i say this is because they must be hard up, for they signed DangerMouse! JESUSFUCKINGCHRISTALMIGHTY

So within the last couple of months our demo has been pirated, recorded, and discussed between all the seattle SCENE luminaries. and the Dude Johnathan Poneman (remember the guy who called me when you were over the last day?) MR Big-money inheritance, right hand man of Bruce Pavitt. and also SUB POP Records financial investor, got us a show at the vogue on a sub pop sunday. Big Deal. but i guess hype and regularly being played on KCMU probably helped, the amount of people who came to Judge us. Not be at a bar, get drunk, watch some bands & have fun. But just watch the showcase event. 1 hr. We felt there was a representative from every seattle band there just watching ————➔

# OH OUR LAST AND FINAL NAME IS NIRVANA

ooH eeerie mystical Doom

We felt like they should have had score cards. And so After the set Bruce excitedly shakes our hands and says "wow Good job let's do A Record". ~~███████~~ then flashes of cameras go off And this Girl from <u>BAcklash</u> says "Gee can we do an interview?" Yeah sure why not. And then people say Good job you Guys are GReAt And NOW we're expected to be total socialites. meeting people, introducing etc. **FUck Im iN High School AGAiN!** ~~I want to move back to Aberdeen.~~ NAH olympiA is just As boring and I can proudly say ive only been in the Smithfield About 5 times this year. And So because of this Zoo-event weve At least gotten A contract for

3 song → A single to be put out by end of August and an EP out

in Sept or oct. We're gonna try to talk them into An LP.

NOW Johnathan is our mAnager, he gets us shows remotely in Oregon & Vancouver. He's pAying for All recording & distribution costs & now we don't have to have outrageous phone Bills. Dave is working out OK. Sometime next year sub pop is gonna have A CARAVAN of 2 or 3 SeAttle Bands go on tour. yeah well see. ~~██~~ Thru your pAst experiences Do you think it would be wise to demant receipts for recording, pressing costs?

eNough About Records oH except this one night last month, Chris And I dropped Acid And we were watching the late show (rip off of Johnny CArson) And PAul Revere and the RAiders were on there, they were so fucking Stupid! DAncing Around with moustaches, trying to Act comical And Goofy.

It reAlly pissed us off and I Asked Chris Do you have Any PAul Revere & the Raiders Albums?

**YEAH** punctuation, I was stoned a lot when I was learning that stuff.

He said yeah, so I looked thru his Big collection and found the Revere Records and Busted them. And he got mad, then he laughed and I searched three the rest of the Row and found Eagles, Carpenters, **Yes**, Joni Mitchell and said with frustration, "What in the fuck do you own these for? And so throughout the Rest of the night we busted about 250 shitty Chris Novoselic Records. not only did we clear more space in the living room, chris declared that he feels cleansed and revitalized.

I don't hang around with Ryan or the other Aberdonians but when im in town I'll get your Sound Garden Record for you. We still make movies, the last one we did was in Tacoma at NEVER NEVER LAND. it's a surrealistic fantasy story book place for Kids, and we made shelli wear a mask of chers head cut out of an album and dance around by big mushrooms and buttfuck the wolf bending over to blow down the three little pigs house. Other stars included Rick Derringer and John lennons Penis. <u>No</u> comment on Matts band MUDHONEY just to be on the safe side. Speaking of safe sides my girlfriend Tracy now has a Brand New "88" Toyota ~~corrolla~~ Turcell, a microwave, food processor, Blender, and an espresso machine, I don't have a job until next month thru TYSS youth service in a printshop Part time. I AM A Totally pampered spoiled Bum Next letter will be less boring about Record deals and ~~~~more stupid drivel Goodbye Dale write soon.

The first song on the Demo is no longer played it is sickening and Dumb. Destroy it it is evil. in the likes of white snake and Bon Jovi

The late 1980's.

This is a subliminal example of
a society that has sucked & fucked
itself into a Rehashing. Value
of greed.

Subliminal in a sense that
there are no p-Rock Collages
of Michael J Fox Reaming Bruce
SPRingsteen clinging to a missile.
instead you get the overall feeling that
you paid WAY too much for

you may say literally Nothing stimulating
yeah but other than the Xerox the layout has a
sense of professionalism

Bull. the Jokes on you
so
Kill Yourself

No amount of effort can save you from

oblivion.
Power Vomit Magazine
No Address
No Editor
No Ad Rates

LOOK →

soundtrack to HR Puffnstuff
featuring MOMMA CASS
and JACK Wilde

Marlen Deitritch sings
Lilly marlene ←

hard-t

C
Blin
Som
WAS
iri
AA
And
the
or
And
em
And
li
Blo
BAC
Doc
Jelly
m
fee
to

An
Ye

F 4
(moveable)

Bar        F 6 (moveable)

Bar        F 7 (moveable)

7

We Are willing to pay
for the majority of
pressing of 1000 copies of
our LP, And All of the
recording Costs.    We
basically just want to
be on your label.
     Do you think you could
PLEASE!  Send us A reply
of Fuck off,  or NOT interested
So we don't have to waste
more money sending more tapes?
thanks.              N pear
NIRUANA.

# NIRVANA

|  |  |  |  |  |  |
|---|---|---|---|---|---|
|  |  |  |  |  |  |
|  |  |  |  |  |  |
|  |  |  |  |  |  |
|  |  |  |  |  |  |
|  |  |  |  |  |  |
|  |  |  |  |  |  |
|  |  |  |  |  |  |
|  |  |  |  |  |  |
|  |  |  |  |  |  |

_____

_____

_____

they werent as gross as G.G. Allin but they
Held their own to say the least. The tension
grew because of a Delay with the P.A. which
Helped the Release of tension when the first
couple of notes of school were struck,
people instantly Rocked back and forth with
eyes closed & beers clenched then
spilt. 5 Roadie friends had to lock arms
behind the P.A. Cabinets & Rocking back & forth
in a wave
pushing the crowd in hopes that the band
wouldn't get hurt. But they did.
Kurdt the vocalist & Guitarist screamed
his last scream to the 2nd song then
Bam the crowd smacked the mike
into his mouth. Blood oozed from his
lip but they instantly started floyd the barber.
After wiping Kurts face, Chris the bass
player accidentally hit Kurt in the eye
with His Bass Headstock it wasn't too
deep at first until Kurt Rammed his
Head into the wall next to him in
protest. it opened more. So Kurdt
took his guitar & hit Chris straight in
the mouth causing a big cut lip. By now
they were pretty Bloody, Chris looking worse
and with only one wound. they were obviously
becoming dizzy and were in pain. but
proceeded to play the set quite out of
tune

# Mead

If You READ
You'll Judge

# the Spiral®
# notebook
11 In. x 8½ In. 70 Sheets
College Ruled
06540
The Mead Corporation, Dayton, Ohio 45463

20    School Zones
25    Street of Cities & towns
50    County ROADS
55    HighwAY

**PASS** within **200** ft of Approaching car

**Follow 20** ft for Every **10.** mph

**TURN** SIGNAL **100** ft before

Lane use Signals

No      Yes
use     use

state     Federal     interstate

4 WAY           Cross
INTERSECTION    ROAD
                Right
                        Cross
                        ROAD        Abrupt
                        Left        end
                                    of ROAD      Y intersection

Divided         ends    ends    two     merge    clearance
HighwAY                         WAY

**PARK wheels DownHill TowArds curb**
12 inches legal park from curb

Speed
  Highway  55
  Cities Towns  25
  School Zones  20
  County Roads  50

PASS within 200 ft of approaching car

Turn Signal on 100 ft before turning

Follow 20 ft for every 10 m.p.h.

STATE FEDERAL     State     interstate

CROSSROAD to Left    Y intersection    Abrupt end    Cross ROAD to Right    4 WAY intersection

merge    TWOLANE ROAD    DiViDED Highway    CLEARANCE    end of DiViDED Highway

PARKing
TURN Wheels TOWARDS curb when PARKing
        DownHill    12 in. AWAY from Curb
  20 ft from intersection    36 Signs Li...

14

Dave,                              5-29-88

    A band needs to practice, in our opinion, at least 5 times a week if the band ever expects to accomplish anything.

    We're tired of total uncertainty every time we play a show, we think..."Are we going to suck"? "Are we tight yet"? We have shows and we don't practice! The two main reasons are, Chris and his work and you and your location. Chris can eventually alter his work schedule and at least practice every week night.

    When we started with you, you claimed you could make it up 4 times a week and would move up here by July or August and it would be no problem for you. We were very hesitant to ever try this because of our experience with driving back and forth to Aberdeen and we knew it would eventually get on your nerves.

    We don't blame you at all for being tired of driving, and we realize what a problem and hassle it is to get someone else to drive you up, but even if you could make it up every day we don't start until 8:30 or 9:00, which is not enough time to even go through the set. We know how long it takes to build a house and you won't move up here as soon as you have claimed, and in our morals and values, fixing up a race car isn't half as important as getting to practice or recording or touring.

                                →

We also aren't convinced that you would get time off, or quit your job next winter to go on tour. The overall aspect of this situation is nothing more than selfish. Getting a name on a record isn't shit. Anybody can do it, but theres a big difference between credentials & notoriety, and self respect through music.

Instead of lying to you by saying we're breaking up or letting this go any further we have to admit that we've got another drummer. His name is Chad, he's from Tacoma and he can make it to practice every night. Most importantly, we can relate to him. lets face it, you are from a totally different culture. Our hobbies and interests are different, and a band can't be a unit unless all the members are compatible. We have really appreciated your loyalty and dedicated attempt at keeping this band alive. You're a great drummer and we hope you pursue another band very soon. We expect you to be totally pissed off and hate our guts and we don't blame you, because this is very sudden and we have not tried to warn you that this was happening. This is not your fault. It's ours. We should have known it wouldn't work, but your enthusiasm and clear headed thinking made us want to try it. and we feel →

5-29-88

really shitty that we don't have the guts to tell you in person. *But we didn't know how mad you would get.* All the luck to you and Laney and your drumming career. And if you wouldn't mind, we would like to suggest to other bands looking for drummers to check you out because your talent shouldn't go to waste.

please let us know when it is in your conbenience for us to bring your drums & mic down. When you want to discuss this ~~with~~ us call. Sorry.
Kurt
chris

P.S. Lani - Thanks for driving Dave up all the time - I know what an awful drive it is. Shelli & I enjoyed spending time with you while they were practicing. Call us sometime & we can get together and do something.

- Tracy & Shelli

J.F.K.: the lamest excuse ever, retrogression
revolve                                           transpose
reverted            Reversion relapse

botanical    such High expectations, so much support,
growing      every one wants it more than me.  Almost feel
             like doing it for them, Such high Aspirations,
             infinity doesnt exist. mathematics are based on 10.
             a numbers of speed numeral variations eventually turn synthesis
of           retrogression, such being: reactive, cause and
             effect, communicational and scenario social interplay
             with situations among people, music, sports,
             war and regional determination of botanical possibilities.  Herbacious
             Hi, I dont have Dyslexia.  An infared light
             will simulate the sun in times of winter.
             A hypnotherapist will hold your hand and aid
             you into going back to bed. Downers & heroin
             make you itch.  If you talk to a friend, the
             friend will offer you a list of remedies that
             youve already tried.  The first seven years of
             my life were amazing, incredible, realistic and
             an absolute grateful joy.
                                              ignore
             To be positive at all times is to erase all important
             and valueble that is important, sacred or valueble.
                                                  be
             To be negative at all times is to threatened
             by your rediculousness and instant discredibility.
rediculous      To translate opinions in an obvious search
manner       for proof of intelligence in the menor of abusive
             use with obscure descriptive words is A desperational
expression   will to sincere, yet retarded expression.

                                        sense
             I feel there is a universal only that amongst
             our generation that everything has been said
             and done.  True.     but who cares
it could     it could still be fun to pretend.
             This is the first decade since the early 1940's that
             two generations listen to & share the same music.
                    (the old school and new school)

18

Dear mark,
Hello. It sounds as If [sure]
everything is working out With Donna,
I cant wait to see & hear the
results! Well i finally have
heard Almost All of your Albums
except All of the beathappening/Trees EP
I hope you dont mind but I
recorded them on the dreadful
CAssetle TAPe. which is something
Im kind of Against people doing, because
it's not supporting the band. but
I swear! If I ever get A job Im
sure I'll buy All the records.
~~mostly do do the test one~~
Well, on the back of the Clashs 1st LP
it says: home taping is killing the
music business 📼 oh! wow.
This stuff on the tape is some 4trk
[sound]
mello pretty, sleep music, weve been
doing for the past couple of months.
It's obvious that it has been inspired
from beat happening/ young MaRBLe giAnts music.
If you like some of it or if you have
something of your own in which you thought
I would be Appropriate for ~~the~~ Collaborating
then Im willing.

~~Hopefully~~ ~~we~~ NIRVANA is planning on
Asking Calvin if he wants to put out A
(IC) Cassette of these songs & A couple
obscure heavy songs too.

   because ~~we're~~ we feel like we're
not Accomplishing Anything by
playing the Seattle Club circuit
& It turns out that our single will
be out in Oct. (Love buzz - b/, cheese)
but there isn't much hope for An EP
within the near future, for Sub POP
is having financial problems  and the
promise of An EP & LP within the year
was just A bullshit excuse for Johnathan
to keep us ~~from taking that~~ from
scouting other lAbels. & So   here it is
  8 months later & we finally put out
A damn single. We've sent the demo
to A few lAbels. but no Response.

   So if you have any numbers
or Addresses or if you meet someone
& give them A demo It would be
greatly Appreciated. we have About
30 bulk recording tapes & Any postage
& handling will be gladly paid.
We just feel like we're becoming stagnant
in Olympia with no record.

Just before I fall asleep and
when I'm really bored I... lay down and
think for a while until I ~~subconciously go~~ fall
into a ~~typing~~ semi hypnotic state of sub-
-conciousness, some call it daydreaming, some
call it just fucking spacing out. but i feel like
I'm not here and it doesn't matter because I'm
sick of putting myself in boring situations and
~~pre~~ fragmentary conversations., just every day
basic sit com happenings, some call it thinking
but when im ~~think I forget to think~~ in this
particular state of mind i forget to think and it
becomes strictly observatory. I notice things
very sensitively like if i focus really hard
I can see small transparent blotches of
~~dirt~~ debris on the outer shell of my eyes.
(or the conjunctiva). And can only follow it
as my eye moves downward, it's like, watching
film footage of amoeba or jelly like
plankton under a microscope. and when
I close my eyes and look up to the sun
the bright orange redness radiates an
intense picture of blood cells or what I
think are blood cells, and they are moving
very rapidly and again I can only focus for
so long before my eyes strain and I have
to look away from the sun into a pillow
and rub my eyes hard then I see some call them stars
Tiny spheres of sparkling light which only
stay for a second then as my eyes focus →

Again ~~things~~ amongst the water or tears
from rubbing I open then look up to
the sky ^AWAY FROM THIS SUN^ And forget About stupid fucking
little squiggly things moving on the outer
layer of my eyes or the ~~B~~ close up
Blood cells in my eye lids And I
stare At the ~~clouds~~ ^SKY^ with perrifial
vision and not trying but just ~~in~~
happening to make out All kinds of
~~faces~~ objects statues in the clouds
And I can do the same with
the wood Grain of the panelling
on my walls. ~~And so what.~~
once I saw jesus on
A Tortilla shell.

UNCERTAINTY like opening your eyes wide in the dark then closing them hard then open and blinded by the sparkling silver dots created from pressure on the corneas, squint, roll, focus, then your blind again but at least you saw light somehow.. maybe ~~it was stored~~ the light was stored in the sockets or held in the iris or clung to the tips of all the nerves and veins. Then your eyes close again and an artificial light appears before the eyelids, probably just a light bulb or a blow torch! jesus its hot! my lashes and brows are curling up and melting emiting the worst smell of burnt hair and thru in my eyelids the red transparency of the light I can see a close up view of blood cells move as I move my eyes back and forth like footage of a documentary of amoeba and plankton jelly like ~~see~~ thru life forms moving man they must be small I cant feel them my eyes must be able to see things MORE clearly than ~~I had~~ expected it's like a microscope but it doesnt matter anymore cause they set me on fire now yep Im sure of it Im on fire God damn it.

3 cups Quick oATs
lArge Bowl

in Sauce pan
2 sticks butter ½ cup milk
2 cups sugar  3 tbs cocoa
¼ tsp salt  2 tsp vanilla
                extract
rolling boil 2 minuts
pour over oAtS stir
until they set

wAx paper

in which,
I felt that
she ~~needs~~

① One of many ways manipulated ~~the~~ circumstances
and reversed the guilt onto me ~~in the way, to~~

① I felt that when she would make an attempt to call
a relative or friend for advice she would always ~~choose~~ these
times when I was around in the house within hearing ~~distance~~
distance. to make it apparently clear that she is concerned "~~quite~~ I dont know
what to do with him, I care so much. He plays guitar and he plays it really good,
but thats all he wants to do, He needs ~~just~~ a dose of reality and to
realize that he needs something to FALL BACK ON!

In a last attempt to make it clear ~~how~~
that this girl did not have downs syndrome
or a monyoloid, ~~the~~ there is proof that ~~[crossed out]~~ Lakeside High school
does not ~~have~~ or ever has had the facilities to
~~teach~~ teach those cronic retards, ~~and~~ in fact Darrin,
Ace, and Trevor were also in one of her classes
& she also had regular classes for normal people.
   A lot of naive asshole kids just called her
retarded because she never talked. ~~which to~~
~~you will find out later in the story how our~~
~~association with her was ~~so~~ badly labeled~~
~~& mistaken~~

   The object of the guys who had been
going there for the past month was to steal
booze from the down stairs basement den..
while ~~one~~ others distracted her by opening
cupboard doors & pretending to eat all the
food, one would go down & take a 5th
& then exit out the downstairs.
   It was basically a gift to Trevor the
pot overlord who enjoyed pot not quite as much
as booze, and to his helpers & I a
reward of getting high in the woods near
the school was always promised if we
stold booze for him.   Only being stoned
within that week for the first few times was
what I claimed as "something I will do
for the rest of my life!") And I would practically
do anything to ensure my supply of the fantastic
weed ~~pot~~.   So we did this routine every other day
   & got away with it for ~~quite a long~~
about a month            ⟹

And during that month I happened to be the
Epitomy of my mental abuse from my mother.
~~The terrible terrible terrible~~
~~before.~~    It turned out that pot didn't
help me escape my troubles too well any more
And I was actually enjoying doing rebellious
things like stealing this booze & busting
store windows getting in fist fights etc....
& nothing even mattered.    I decided within
the next month I'll not sit on my roof and
think about jumping but ill actually kill myself
And I wasnt going out of this world without
actually knowing what it is like to get laid.
    So one day after school I went to
her house alone, and invited myself in
And she offered me some twinkies and I sat
on her lap and said "let's fuck" And I
touched her tits And she went into her bedroom
And got undressed in front of me with the
door open And I watched & realized that
it was actually happening so I tried to
fuck her but didnt know how and asked her
if she had ever done this before And she said
a lot of times mainly with her cousin.
    I got grossed out very heavily with how
her vagina smelled & her sweat reaked so
I left.    My concience grew to where I
couldnt go to school for a week And when i
went back I got in-house suspection in the
office for skipping And that day the girls
father came in screaming & accusing someone
of taking advantage of his daughter

& they went in the ~~off~~ principals office And yelled At eachother & they came out with a yearbook & were going to have her pick me out. but she couldn't because I ~~was~~ didn't show up for pictures that year. & so during lunch the rumors started And by the next day she told my name And everyone was waiting for me to yell & cuss & spit At me calling me the retard ~~fucker~~'.

Because a lot of people liked me the sides were even but I couldn't handle the ridicule so on a saturday night I got high & drunk & walked down to the train tracks & layed down & waited for the 11:00 train & I put 2 big pieces of cement on my chest & legs & the train came closer & closer.

And it went on the next track beside me instead of over me. So I rode the bus to ~~Lakeside school~~ from ~~Jenkins Lane~~ every day pretending to go to school & doing acid instead walking in the woods, so my mom would think I was going to school & the cops stopped me one night at a football game & I went down to the station & they tape recorded my confession of what I did and said that ~~her~~ family can't do anything, because she was 18 And not mentally retarded. But tension from school made me have to attent ~~Jenkins~~ school And the train scared me enough to try to rehabilitate myself & my guitar ~~seemed to~~ playing seemed to be improving so I became less manically depressed but still never had any friends because I hated everyone for they were so phony.

NIRVANA is from Olympia WA, 60 miles from Seattle. NIRVANAS Guitar/vocalist (Kurt Kobain) And Bass-(Chris Novoselic) lived in Aberdeen 190 miles from Seattle.

Aberdeens population consists of Highly bigoted Redneck-snoose chewing- deer shooting, ~~faggot~~ killing- logger types who "Aint to ~~~~ partial to weirdo New Wavers!" (Chad) drums is from An island of Rich Kid-L.S.D Abusers.

NIRVANA is A trio who play Heavy Rock with Punk overtones.

They usually dont have jobs.

So they can tour anytime.

NIRVANA HAS never jammed on Gloria, or Louie Louie. NOR have they ever had to Re write those songs & call them their own.

NIRVANA is looking to put their music to Vinyl or Accepting A loan of About $2,000.00.

Kurdt

<u>Lance Link</u>
After Best happening

Crybaby & Richard Simmons

Hot Dog eating contest

* Penis Balloon insertion
   for erection

* light bulb swallower
     Rem
     H Rollins
     L Lunch
     Tards
   Bill murray lounge
   Stairway to Heaven

* DAVEY & GoliAth
   Bros QUAY
   Spoons magnets BABY

* monster tard movie

Jesse Hello,

Believe me, I have purposely been
delaying writing you for a while so
when our single finally comes out I
could send it to you as well as a letter.
But God time flys and sub pop
is broke and full of shit. And I didn't
realize how long its been since I
received your letter. So I'm sorry!

Hey cheer up dude, your letter
sounded like you're kinda bored.

I can't wait until you come down
for christmas, it will be the most
exciting ~~$~~ event this year. We got
our test pressings back for the single, I've
been waiting for so long that I'm not
even ~~worried about~~ looking forward to it coming out. We've
refused to do anything else with sub pop
even though they really want us to put out an
EP. We've decided to put out our own
LP. We found a record pressing plant that
will press 1000 records for $1,600.00. So at
$8.00 a piece we only have to sell about
250 records to get our money back, and
the rest is pure profit, then all we
have to do is find a distributor.

We played with the Butthole surfers. And
then D.O.A in seattle. The melvins are coming
back to play a couple shows with us.

Chris and shelli broke up. God am I
relieved! she is still living in Tacoma

And Chris is temporarily staying in Aberdeen for free at his moms. I'm very content with the relationship Chris, Chad and I have, We get along great and have a lot of dedicated fun. We are becoming very well received in Seattle & other places in Wash. Promoters call us up to see if we want to play, instead of us having to Hound people for shows. Its now just a matter of time for labels to hunt us down, now that we've promoted ourselves pretty good by doing small Remote tours. OK. enough about the Band.

I've got a janitor job, working with this older guy cleaning 4 restaurants. Pays cash under the table part time.

Tracy and I get along just fine, as usual. Lately Ive found myself becoming lazy. I hardly write any stories and I dont work on songs quite as intently as in the past. You know why? ??

Television Television is the most evil thing on our planet.

Go Right now to your TV and toss it out the window, or sell it and buy a better stereo. I have the flu Right now so I dont feel like conjuring up witty literature. my eyes burn & when I fart, hot bubble acid ooze squirts from my

Greetings,

NIRVANA is a three piece spawned from the bowels of a Redneck loser town called ~~of~~ Aberdeen WA. and ~~the~~ hippie commune ~~from~~ Bainbridge Island. Only together for 7 months Kurdt – Guitar vocals – Chris bass & Chad – Drums have acquired a single on Sub Pop Records (*a song in Sub Pop 200 comp,*) A Demo, success & fame & a following of millions, selling their bottled sweat & locks of hair have proven to be the largest money maker so far, but futurei dolls, peechees, lunchboxes & bed sheets are in the works. AN LP is due ~~this~~ April from the wonderful ~~head~~ offices of Sub Pop World headquarters. talent Agents bruce Pauitt (alias Henry Mancini) and Jonnathan Poneman (alias fred flintstone) have "treated the boys good" the boys hope to work on more projects in the ~~future~~. with them

NIRVANA sounds like black sabbath - playing the KNACK, Black flag, led Zeppelin, & the stooges, with a pinch of Bay City Rollers. their musical influences are: H.R. Puffnstuff, ~~Spider~~ Marine Boy, Divorces, Drugs, Sound effects Records, the Beatles, Young marble giants, slayer, leadbelly, IGGY, NIRVANA sees the underground music SEEN as becoming, stagnant and more Accessible towards commercial MAJOR LAbel interests. Does NIRVANA want to change this? No way! We want to CASH IN & suck butt up to the big wigs in hopes that we too ~~cam~~ get High & fuck wax figure- hot babes, who will be required to have A certified Aids test 2 weeks prior to ~~the~~ day of handing out back stage passes. Soon we will need chick spray Repellant. Soon we will be coming to your town & Asking if we can stay at your house & use your Stove. Soon we will do encores of Gloria & louie louie at benefit concerts with All our celebrity friends.

We Realize that there ~~was~~ once A 60's band called NIRVANA but dont get us ~~confused~~ with them because they totally Suck Big fucking Dick.

N Pear olympia W 98500

Good Bye.

"SAFER THAN HEAVEN"

NIRVANA

GREETINGS,

NIRVANA is a three piece spawned from the bowels of a redneck - logger town called Aberdeen WA, and a hippie commune on Bainbridge island.

Although only together for seven months KurDt-guit-voc, Chris-bass and Chad-drums have acquired a single on Sub Pop records, one cut on the Sub Pop 200 compilation, a demo, an LP in April, success,fame and a following of millions.

Selling their bottled sweat and locks of hair have proven to be their biggest money makers so far, but in the future: dolls, pee chees, lunch boxes and bed sheets are in the works.

From the wonderful offices of Sub Pop world headquarters our talent agents Bruce Pavitt and Johnathan Poneman have treated the boys good.

NIRVANA hope to work on more projects with them in the future.

NIRVANA sounds like: Black Sabbath playing the Knack, Black Flag, Led ZEP, the Stooges and a pinch of Bay city Rollers.

Their personal musical influences include: H.R Puffnstuff, Marine boy, divorces, drugs, sound effect records, the Beatles, Young Marble Giants, Slayer, Leadbelly and Iggy.

NIRVANA sees the underground music SEEN as becoming stagnant and more accessible towards commercialized major label interests.

Does NIRVANA feel a moral duty to change this cancerous evil?

No way! We want to cash in and suck butt of the big wigs in hopes that we too can GET HIGH and FUCK. GET HIGH and FUCK. GET HIGH and FUCK.

Soon we will need chick repellant spray. Soon we will be coming to your town asking if we can stay over at your house and use your stove.

Soon we will do encores of Gloria and Louie Louie at benefit concerts with all our celebrity friends. NIRVANA c/o SUB POP 1932 1st AVE..#1103. Seattle WA 98101 or

Thank you for your time.

FUCK NOW, SUFFER LATER

GREETINGS,

NIRVANA is a heavy-pop/punk/dirge-combo spawned from the bowels of Seattle Washington.

Although only together for seven months KURDT Guitar/voc, CHRIS-bass, CHAD-drums and JASON-guitar have acquired a single, an LP entitled "Bleach", one cut on the SUB POP 200 compilation, sucess, fame and a following of millions.

Selling their bottled sweat and lochs of hair have proven to be their biggest money makers so far, and in the future: dolls, pee-chees, lunch boxes and bed sheets are in store.

From the towering offices of SUB POP world headquarters, our talent agents Johnathan Poneman and Bruce Pavitt have treated the boys swell.

NIRVANA hope to produce more projects with them in the future.

NIRVANA sounds like mid-tempo-Black Sabbath playing the Knack, Black Flag, the Stooges with a pinch of Bay City Rollers.

Their personal musical influences include: H.R. Puffnstuff, Speed Racer, DIVORCES, drugs, sound effects records, the beatles, rednecks, asorted hard rock, old punk rock, Leadbelly, Slayer and of course the Stooges.

NIRVANA sees the underground SeeN as becoming stagnant and more accessible towards commercialized major label interests.

Does NIRVANA feel a moral duty to change this cancerous evil?

NO way! We want to CASH IN and SucK UP to the big wigs in hopes that we too can GET HIGH AND FUCK GET HIGH AND FUCK.GET HIGH AND FUCK.

SOON we will need groupie repellant spray. SOON we will be coming to your town asking if we can stay over at your house and use the stove. SOON we will do encores of GLORIA and LOUIE LOUIE at benefit concerts with all our celebrity friends.
NIRVANA c/o SUB POP
1932 1st ave. # 1103. Seattle
Wa 98101 or
    Thank you for your time.

S·U·B
P·O·P

MARK,
   WHOA! Polly Perreguin is
my favorite song as of this decade.
I've been soaking up the sounds of
the Screaming Trees for a few
months and ~~——~~ I think its way
better than most, although in the
pop genre I like pixies &
 Smithereens a bit better. But
Polly Perreguin, JEEZUS GOD!
what a complete masterpiece.
 Hey hows tour? oh.   Donna Seems
to fit in  just fine.  I predict
the mighty Major label in the future
for you people.  Heres some well,
fuck, I must admit screaming Trees
influenced pop weve been experimenting
with.    we played with the Butthole Surfers,
they wouldnt move their drums. Jeesus!
Got paid 75.00 whole dollars.
   Sub Pop is always broke.  So were
openly looking for any other offer. They
mean well but we don't feel its fair
for mudhoney to be favored & catered
to a higher level than the other bands.
 Oh well. ~~————————~~ we want
to tour in March. if you have any #'s
or Suggestions, we would appreciate
any Help.

NIRVANA

Dear Kenichewa _____.

**NIRVANA** IS A three piece from the Outskirts of Seattle WA.

Kurdt-Guitar/voice and Chris-bass have struggled with too many un dedicated drummers for the past 3 years, performing under such names As: Bliss, throat Oyster, Pen Cap Ch. Ted ed Fred etc.. for the last 9 months we have had the pleasure to take Chad-drums under Our wings and develop what we are now and always will be **NIRVANA**.

3 regularly broadcasted carts on K.C.M.U (Seattle College Radio also KAOS olympia) Played with: Leaving Trains, Whipping Boy, Hell's Kitchen, Trecherous Jaywalkers & Countless local acts.

Looking for: EP or LP     We have About 15 Songs Recorded on 8 Tracks AT Reciprocal studios in Seattle.

Willing to compromise on material (Some of this shit is pretty old)     Tour Any-time forever] hopefully the music will speak for itself

Please Reply THANK YOU     Area Code (206)

N. PEAR olympia UA. 98506

# Things the band needs to do

① Send some fucking demo tapes get chad to fucking fork over some money.

② PRESS Kit
1) get ahold of charles and Alice to get some pictures
2) have Tam write out a story line
3) then copy them off. Simple!

③ Find a practice place

④ Call NANN WARSAW in chicago. Ask if she has any connections with Touch-n-go Also Ask for ~~a list~~ her to send a list of prominent Magazines & Record stores that we could make contacts with.

⑤

AT <u>EVERY</u> stop you m<u>ust</u> check:

1. OiL
2. WATER
3. Air pressur
4. transmission
5. Batery WATer
6. Brake fluid

7. PACK Bearings
8. check lights
9. lug nuts
10. WASH VAN
11. Radiator Hose
12. Windows

\* LOCK ALL DOORS

<u>NO</u> Guests, groupies, Band members etc.

<u>NO</u> use of Any Gas Corporation services Besides EXXON. NO exceptions

Every 400 miles there will be An inspection check of VAN cleAnliness And equipment count.
Find A sAfe place to pull over And tAke every piece of musical equipment out: refer to <u>musical</u> <s>equip</s>electronic pamphlet in glove compArtment.

42

part time Janitorial position

in the olympian newspaper

7 months at lemons Janitorial
1 year at polynesian condominium resort
in ocean shores
2 summers work at Aberdeen YMCA
& Weathermax High school

& 9 months at lamplighter restaurant
in Grayland WA.

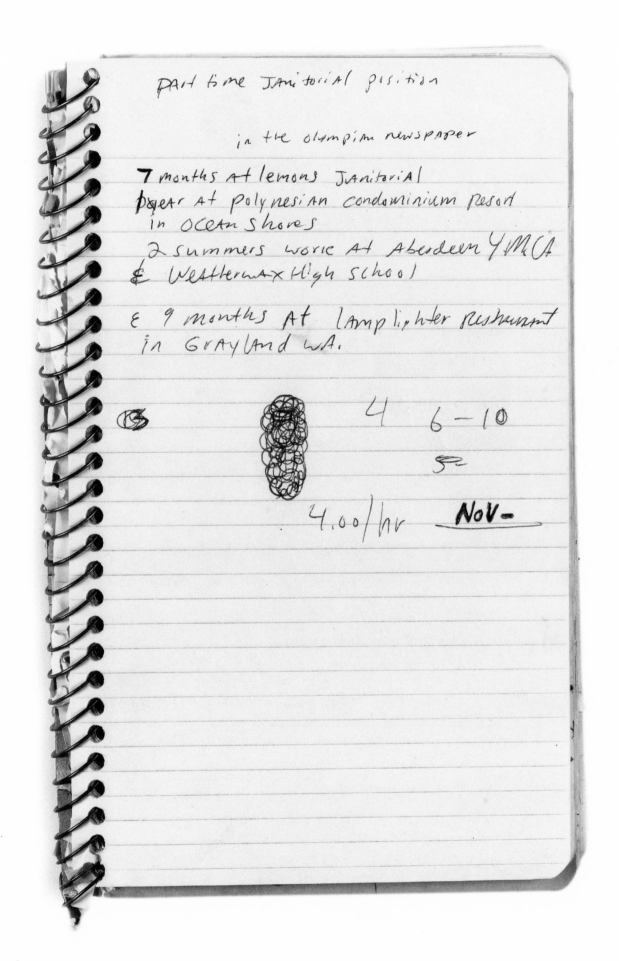

4    6 - 10

4.00/hr        NOV-

$2\frac{1}{2}$ yr's experience

<u>Lemons Janitorial</u>   Sept 87 - Feb 88
Basic Route cleaning buildings  $4.50/hr

<u>Polynesian Condominium</u> hotel Resort   Ocean shores $5.00/hr
Sept - 86 - June 87   c/o Betty Kaales (housekeeping)
~~custodian~~ maintenance ~~help~~   basic odd jobs, windows
carpet cleaning,          moved to olympia

<u>Aberdeen Y.M.CA</u>        c/o Alfie Bensinger  $3.35/hr
~~April~~ MAY 86 - ~~August~~ Sept 86
lifeguard, preschool swimming instructor, day care
baseball coach, maintenance.   Summer temporary employment

<u>Lamplighter Restaurant</u>   grayland WA    $4.25/hr
Sept 85 - March 86   c/o  Bud ~~Turley~~ & Audrey Turley
dishwasher, prep, clean up, busperson

Coast building
10029  So TACOMA WAY
off exit            behind
127      TACOMA Cody's Restaurant

# Pine ~~Fresh~~ Tree
## Janitorial Service

Commercial

Basic commercial maintenance

PINE TREE
Janitorial Service

Kurt    Chris

friendly, prompt,
& clean.

Commercial maintenance

bathrooms - ^sink- toilet - mop - mirrors - Paper towel/
TP-supply.   Office - Dust - vacuum - sweep - ashtrays -
-Garbage - windows -

We purposely limit our number of commercial offices
in order to ~~take time. And personally clean~~
personally clean while taking our time.  We
guarantee $50.00 lower Rates, than your present
Janitorial Service.

You see, other ~~Computer~~ services usually have
too many buildings assigned to the individuals Route:
so in turn they end up Running thru buildings trying
for time.  but At pine tree ———

45

my lyrics are a big pile of contradictions.
they're split down the middle between
very sincere opinions and feelings that I have
and sarcastic and hopefully - humorous
rebuttles towards cliché - bohemian ideals
that have been exhausted for years.
    I mean it seems like there are only two
options for personalities as songwriters either
they're SAd, tragic visionaries like morrisey
or michael Stipe or Robert smith. or there's
the goofy, Nutty white boy, Hey, lets party
and forget everything people like Van Halen
or All that other ~~~~ Heavy maetal crap

    I mean I like to be passionate and
sincere, but I also like to have
fun and act like a dork.
    Geeks unite.

# DOWNER

1
PORTRAY SINCERITY ACT out of LOYALTY
Defend your free Country-wish AWAY PAIN
HAnd OUT Lobotomys to SAVE little familys
Surrealistic fantasy Bland Boring PLAIN

2
Holy NOW IN Restitution - living out our Date-
with FUSION - IN our whole fleece shun in
BASTARD - dont feel guilty mASTer writing

3
Somebody says that their not much like I AM
I Know I CAN - MAKE enough up the words As
you GO Along I SING then some.

4
SickeNING pesimist hypocrite mASTer
Conservative Communist Apocalyptic BASTard
Thank you DEAR GOD for putting me on this EARth
I feel very priviledged IN debt for my thirst


2 and 3

# MR Blew

Now if you wouldn't mind -
I would like to Blew

And if you wouldn't mind - I would
like to lose -

And if you wouldn't care - I would
like to leave -

And if you wouldn't mind ~~of~~ I would
like to breathe

Is there Another Reason for your
Stain?

Could you believe who - we knew
stress and strain

Here is Another word that Rhymes
with shame

You could do ANything

# MR MOUSTACHE.

fill me in on your new vision
WAKE me up with- indecision
Help me trust your mighty wisdom
~~Yes I Eat~~ cow - I Am not proud

~~write down what you want me to see~~
~~I'll erase what youve just shown me~~
~~I don't claim my skin is Righteous~~

~~Mold me into satisfaction~~
~~Milk will keep you strong and healthy~~
~~pat me on the back for~~
~~Hit me if I do whats not sound~~

show me how **you** Question Questions
lead the WAY **to** Righteous scheming
take my han**d** And give it cleaning *to temptation*
~~Now not~~ cow - I Am not proud
yes I eat cow

EAsy in An EAsy chAir
Poop AS hArd AS Rock
I don't like you AnywAys
SeAl it in A box

# floyd the Barber

Bell on Door Clanks - come on in
floyd observes my Hairy chin
sit down chair dont Be Afraid
steamed Hot Towel on my face
   I        WAS        shaved  (3x's)

Barney Ties me to the chair
I cant see Im Really scared
floyd Breathes hard I hear A zip
pee pee pressed Against my lips
   I        w As        shamed (3x's)

I sense others in the Room
Opey Aunt Bee I PResume
they Take Turns in cut me up
I died smothered in Andys Butt

   I        WAS        shaved (3x's)

# PAPER CUTS

when.. my feeding TIME
She push food thru the Door
I crawl towards the CRACKS of Light
Sometimes I can't find my WAY

~~what I get to feed~~

newspapers spread Around
SOAKING All that they Can
A cleaning is due AGAIN
~~INCREASING chances of Rain~~
A Good HOSING DOWN

The LAdy whom I feel A maternal Love for
cannot look me in the eyes. But I see
hers And they Are Blue And they Cock And
Twitch and masturbate

                    I SAID So
~~WHY - Because of~~ - I SAID So - I SAID SO

A REASON     A REASON     A REASON     ~~Try~~ Try AGAIN

BLACK windows Are PAINT
I Scratch with my NAILS
I See others just like me
Why do they NOT Try escape?

They bring out the older ones
They point At my WAY
The older ones Come with lights
And TAKE my family AWAY

CONT.  →

Paper Cuts
Continued

And very later I have learned to accept some
friends of Ridicule - my whole existence was
for your Amusement And that is why Im Here with you

To Take you - with me To - your eyes are Blue
~~Believe~~ Relief to     NIRVANA

    NIRVANA     NIRVANA     NIRUANA

    NIRVANA     NIRVAWA     NIRUANAAAH

# HAIRSPRAY QUEEN

① I WAS your mind • You were my my ene mye
You were mine • I WAS WAS your ene mye
You would mind • I WAS your your ene me
You were mine • I WAS WAS your enA

EARS                    RAN G   2x's
                    ①

② AT Night • the wishfull Goddess • AT Night
Shell Wish the HARDest • AT Night the Disco
Goddess • AT Night the Witch go gosh

①
②
Voice ① DRoned

AT Night • the wishful Goddess • AT Night
Shell Wish the HARDest • AT Night •
the DiSco Goddess • AT Night •
the itch so modest • AT Night •
the Crisco loch Ness • AT Right •
the mouthfull omelette • AT Sight
the fishfull goblets • AT Night the Witch go
GAAAAAAAAAAAWD

53

# Mexican Seafood

AH the itchy flAkes it is A flaming
All the Gels and cremes it is pertAining
to A fungus mold cured by injection
Hope it's only AH A yeAst infection

② OH well it burns when I - it hurts when
I pee - OH well it hurts when I - it hurts
when I see.

Now I vomit cum And diAhrreA
on the tile floor like OAtmeAl pizzA
fill my toilet bowl full of A cloudy puss
I feel the Blood becoming chowder rust

②

Roll into my Bed which does consist of
lice Bugs And fleAs And yellow mucus
stAined dirt VASAline Toe JAm & Booger
stomAch Acid worms thAt DAnce in
sugAred sludge

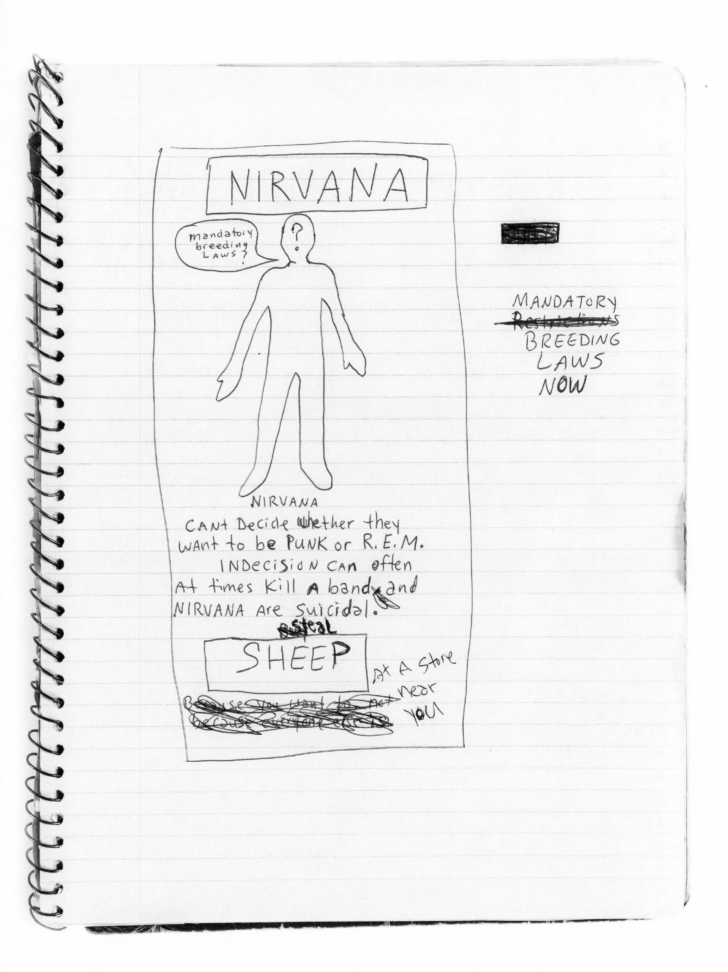

NIRVANA

The KKK are the
only NIGGers.

May women rule
the world.

Abort christ.

Assasinate the
Greater And Lesser
of two evils.

steal
SHEEP

At a store near
you.

NIRVANA

~~10 GRAMMY~~
3 time Granny award winners.
NO. 1 on billbored top 100
for 36 consecutive weaks
in a row.  2 times on
the cover of Bowling stoned,
Hailed as the most original,
thought provoking and important band
of our decade by Thyme & Newsweak

NIRVANA

Flowers
perfume
candy
puppies
Love
Generational
Solidarity
And
Killing Your
parents

SHEEP

# Pen Cap Chew

OH Lesser God OH LoAthe me
OH lesser God OH Your lonely
OH lesser God OH Bore me
OH lesser God OH    OH

You get you get you get you get to me
Holy is the time it's such an easy way to go

You get you get you Get — You get to Be
Hide the Struggle in the Skin under A
    finger nAil

OH lesser god OH loAthe me oH lesser god OH lonely
OH lesser god OH loAthe me oH lesser Doy OH lonely

WAste your time By sAving Worthless Gullables
Kill A Pollitician And then wear his Clothes
this decade is the Age of Re-HAshing
Protest And then go to JAil for Tresspassing
    Go    Home   (4x's)

CAn you see the ReAson for My Entrope
Is there something wrong without Society
Has your Concience got to you for Building
Trends — is that why unoticing you
    EAt your pens?

    Go  Home    (8x's)

# Aeroszeppelin

Whats a season in a Right
If you can't have anything
Whats the reason in a rhyme
If a plan means anything
Whats the meaning in a crime
its a fan if anything
Wheres a leaning in a line
its A BRAND  its A Brand ████████

How a culture comes again
it was all here yesterday
And you swear its not a trend
Doesn't matter anyways
theyre only here to talk to friends
Nothing new is everyday
You█ could shit upon the stage  they'll be fans
if you Brand  if you Brand  if you Brand

All the kids will eat it up -
if its packaged properly
steal a sound and imitate
keep a format equally
not an ode
just the facts
Where our world is nowadays
An idea is what we lack
it doesn't matter anyways

58

# MELVINS

I remember painfully        you
                                        saucy upstart

Gyuto monks

if you need an explanation on what montsano
is like, refer to any NIRVANA article of the past
3 years on the subject of Aberdeen, the two
coastal logging slums are similar in the lack of
cultural          and ~~music~~ good musical availability

I'm tired of people saying the melvins don't get the recognition they deserve

melvins when they finally get the recognition they deserve

they can look forward to ~~least~~ un punk rock adoration

~~detractors~~ (late) from fans waiting outside the venue waiting for autographs

the true adoration that matters is one they have already
by the small amount of fanatics who are into them already

I remember when the melvins played Jimi Hendrix & Cream songs
~~hell they weren't the melvins~~ then

them festival

I remember: when the melvins played lightning speed melodic,
punk rock hardcore ~~a~~ with typewriter drumming.
then they
~~then they played~~ started slowing down with a mix of stultus

Black flag damage II

~~of~~ melodic sabbath like abrasion

       excitedly
~~Buzz~~ Buzz came over with Blackflags MY WAR
~~claiming this is the best~~ claiming it was ~~the best~~ as important
as

59

. their habit was financed by their earnings of pizza & bus boy jobs

During the Summer month of the U.S. festival in 84

I remember in the summer of 82 or 83 there was this extravaganza of a rock-like woodstock concert held in some far away exotic land featuring all the contemporary Hard rock acts like AC DC or Van Halen. To the stoner world it was a big deal but for me it was something a joke I didn't pay much attention to it but I remember my friends staring up to the sky during the weeks prior to this gathering with so fear empty unstoppable of empty dreams that this festival is never to be the smoker shed reality. in other words there wasn't a chance in hell that they'll save up enough pot money to make the long trek to the fatherland promise land of the U.S festival

I remember hanging out at montesano Washingtons thriftway when this short haired employee employee boxboy who kinda looked like the Guy in Air Supply handed me a flyer that reads. the Them festival. tomorrow night in the parking lot behind Thriftway

free live Rock music

Montesano Washington a place not accustomed to having live rock acts in their little village   A population of a few thousand loggers and their subservient wives

~~I~~ showed up with stoner friends in a van
we pulled into the parking lot behind the
Thriftway ~~Aother zombies~~ slouch bobbed with combes in their back pockets ~~congested~~ ~~above~~
~~it~~ There stood the Air supply box boy ~~with~~
~~a fuck this~~ holding a les Paul with A picture
from A magazine of kool cigarettes lamenated on it a mechanic
red headed biker boy and that "lukin guy", the first
to ever wear skin tight levis, a bold and brave
change from stickan finger or Sanfrancisco riding Gear.

They played faster than I had ever imagined
music could be played and with more energy than
my iron Maiden records could provide, this
was what I was looking, for, AH punk Rock
The other stones were Bored and ~~kept~~
~~asking them~~ kept shouting, play some
Def Leppard. God I hated those fucks more
than ever I came to the promise land
of A Grocery store I, found my special purpose the next day I
spiked ~~my~~ the upper part of my head, but
I couldn't quite part with my stoner roots and the long hair in
the back, thus developing the first Bi level
haircut in montesano history, I walked around
for a week looking like rod stewart. I started
following the melvins around, I was the
quiet tag along. one day they even let
me try out for the band but I was

way too nervous ~~and~~ So I sat in the corner at hundreds of melvins practices during the next few years as I watched buzz transform from typewriter drumming, speed core to the constepation blues stemmed from the influence of Black flag, my war, ST Uitus and a short lived stint with various metal Blade recording artists. something new was H muslim transforming Buss do this

thru a few years of ~~study~~ internally personal developments of strict morals and opinions niche like sincere devotion to the celebration of ~~of~~ energy and the appreciation of spirituality ~~and sincere~~ Buzz stays true to his school. giving off an air of if you even think of me compromising Ill kill you attitude rolling his ~~eye~~ eyes to the back of the head Narcoleptic epileptic little Boy rocking back n forth disease? pissing sweat in A ritually Autistic sway downstroking muffled lowest notes possible chunk chopping block, Guttural bowel drones. harmonic satanic and uh heavy. low Deep cool man cool Goddamn the pusher man. A lot of mohawks said I used to like the melvins until they became Black Sabbath Jeez ~~that~~ A typically clever observation

# The MeLVINS Are alive

WORDS suck.  I mean, every thing has been said.  I cant remember the last real interesting conversation ive had in a long time.  WORDS arent as important as the energy derived from music, especially live.  I dont think ive ever gotten any good descriptions from lyric sheets, except WHITE ZOMBIE whos lyrics remind me that theres only so many words in the English language, and most good imagery has been used, as well as good band names, LP titles and not to mention the bloody music itself.  GEE, I dont want to sound so negative but were dealing with the MELVINS.  IN one live MELVINS performance you wont be able to understand very many words, as is with any band) but you will FEEL the negative ENERGY.  Music is ENERGY.  A mood, atmosphere.  FEELING.  The MELVINS have and always will be the king pins of EMOTION.  Im not talking about fucking stupid human compassion, this is one of the only real istic reminders that every day we live amongst VIOLENCE.

There is a time and place for this music.  So if you want to shake your groove thang to simple primal rock, then go see a fucking bar band!  The MELVINS aint for you. And they probably dont want ya.

Like I said im not too hip on lyrics, so I didnt ask them about lyrics.  Aparently their lyrics are almost equally important as the music.  In their case I have to agree, even though I can hardly decipher any of the words, I can sense they display as much emotion as the music and therefore I hypocritically plead to you "BUZZ", On the next record have a lyric sheet, and if you need, have an explanation for every line.  Im shure a lot of kids would dig it.  man.

Speaking of BUZZ, he looks better in an afro than that guy in the movie CAR WASH.  Im thinking he should take advantage of this blessing and be the first to go beyond the hip hops shaved symbols and architectured genious of scalp artistry and SCULPt a wacky far out cactus or Bull Winkle antlers.

He writes the songs, riffs first, lyrics second and goddamn is they good!  Hes an all around nice guy.

DALE lost weight, bleached and chopped his hair.  He plays even harder and an all around NICE GUY.

LORI kicks John Entwistles butt, and is all around nice guy.

They enjoy the GYUTO MONKS , Tibetan Tantric choir.

One of the only forms of religious communication in which I have been emotionally affected by along with the MELVINS and uh maybe the STOOGES or SWANS raping a slave EP'.  The only good thing MICKEY HART ever did was to bring this sacred group of monks on a tour in which ive heard from many, seemed like an impersonal circus or freak show. Oh well they needed money to build a new monestary. They probably didnt notice the yochie dead heads hanging out in the audience. yuk!

The special technique in the monks vocalization is a long study of producing three notes or a full chord in the form of long droning chants.  It makes for a soothing eerie feeling.

**This is an interview** that was written several months After matt left the Band in so oct"

are you satisfied with the new line up of the melvins. and where you live?

are you ~~tired~~ sick and tired of people asking about the recent breakup with matt and A rumored wedding?

what do you see in this picture? →

where do you work?

is pizza your favorite food?

is it possible to drive A stick shift in S.F.?

Are you experimenting with electronic drums?

to hell with your influences, what's A list of stuff youre listening to lately?

whos your favorite band?

who?
NO. REALLY?
what do you think of the "seattle sound"?
HAVE you heard the new Die kreuzen album?

Are you planning on coming to Seattle or its
surroundings areas to play a few show?
How many shows have you played in S.F. or its surrounding area?
Whats the crowd response?

Do you think that the Album Gluey Porch Treatments
Actually exists or maybe there were only 15
printed up?

I think the Album would sound even heavier on
A dance club sub woofer sound system in A
Euro Disco fag bar.
what do you think?

What really cool toys do you have?

do you think born again is A good BLACK SABBATH ALBum?

did you know that C/Z is collaborating with Toxic Shock
& they have an Add in some fanzines and amongst others BANDS
your 7" inch is listed?

wouldnt it be nice to walk into a store and
find a Melvins Record?

Are your song writing styles changing in any WAY? or
can we expect the same product forever from the melvins?

I didn't think so.

Tell me a story:

Now you Ask me A question And I will
Respond with this

Thanks for the interview
We hope to see you sometime
          cheer i - o

**Dale,**

Kenichewah,

OKAY, I have not lost my soulful, imbeded roots as an honorary punk Rock, hard, heavy, Gunka Gunka Gunka music slut. Nor have I been sucking up the cute, innocent and clean image Olympia has to offer either, but I have learned to appreciate some of this Calvin/simplistic stuff enough to do my own rendition, which is actually something I've been planning on doing for years, so it's not really a rip off or a ~~influence~~ borrowed influence. I'm making up excuses because I don't think you'll like it, but I sent you it anyhow just to fill up space, ~~after~~ I don't have much new music to let you hear. So anyways..
"How the Hell ARE you doing dale crover master of DRUMS?"

Send me boom box stuff NOW! I don't think too many people will think you guys will suck, like you said the leg worshipping whores might, but B. F. D!

Chris and I were wandering Around the CAMPUS one SAturday evening, and we CAme Across this band playing. Inside we found 3 greeners jamming on bAd psychedellic blues, because thats what Greeners do on Saturday evenings. They showed us their new $200.00 worthless whammy pieces of shit KRAmers & New Laney Amps, I wasn't impressed. And then over in the corner I noticed A left handed late 60's fender mustang. After swallowing my puke I calmly Asked if they wanted to sell it and they said...
"Oh that _old_ piece of shit?" "I don't care $50 bucks".

Chris entered the conversation And said.
"I don't know man it's pretty junky." "OK twenty bucks. it's only pawn shop material anyways. It's nothing compared to our new KRAmers.

So Chris and I Ran blindly through a thick forest towards the light and to the van and to a bank machine and bought the pre CBS "65" left handed fender mustang. The END

My Amp blew up. I got 2 more evel knievel motorcycles. Rape man. Rapeman! Rapeman! I don't have any of their stuff on tape yet. probably because they don't have anything out.yet but Rapeman are Steve Albini on guitar/vocals (from Big Black) & the drummer & bass player from Scratch Acid. I saw them last weekend and I think they are one of my favorite bands. I'll have to wait until I hear them on record. but god damn they were fucking cool live!

I defrosted the icebox with a hammer. hours later Tracy noticed an awfully powerful fume & so we thought it was Free-on so we got the animals outside & the fumes became so bad that we couldn't go in the apt at all. it started to burn our skin & so we stayed next door for 1 night & in TACOMA the 2nd night & turns out it wasn't free on but even more of a deadly gas called sulfer dioxide. Its like if you were to fill a bucket of Bleach & Ammonia & tie someones face to it. I left a butter scotch swiss miss pudding out over night & it turned Bright flourescent green. So don't beat on your ice box with a hammer.

I talked to Jesse Again. he's not getting a divorce Anymore, instead he's buying more credit cards.

Touch N Go          scratch Acid
Demo                side of
                    NIRVANA
floyd the barber
Spank Thru
Hairspray Queen
~~Aeroszeppelin~~
Mexican Seafood
BeesWAX
Beans
~~Paper cuts~~
_____

Big cheese
Love Buzz
Aeroszeppelin
~~Paper Cuts~~
pen cap chew
montage of heck

Listed Price/HR                    Call
                                   No price

BASIC TRACK PRODUCTIONS
8-TRACK $15/hr                      BLACKwood Laird
                                   8 track
Tri West Recording
$15/hr 8 TRACK                      michael lord prod.
                                   16 TRACK Recording

Will
Call me
BACK in
A half
Hour          10re  **50** BUCKS Or TAPE        3hrs mix
              SAT   SUN
         by   16    17   All day 9:00
         3:00

         how much per Hour For a 3piece band   weekends this month
                                               About 10 hours
         40 min material                            evening
         half overdubs Guitar vocals               6-10  10
                                                   16 17

                                                24        31

         engineer?
         Located?

         I want to do a master for a pressing

                    american music
              APEX
         half inch  Reel Reel


                   So. side seattle
         SEA TAC Airport
         21040 5th Ave So. Seattle

70

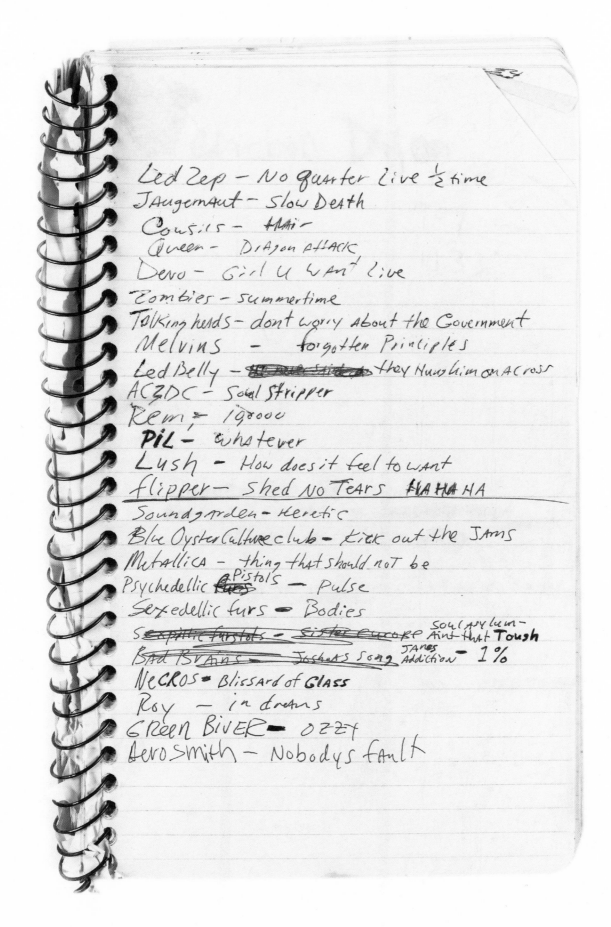

Led Zep — No Quarter Live ½ time
Jaugernaut — Slow Death
Cousins — Hair
Queen — Dragon Attack
Devo — Girl u Want Live
Zombies — Summertime
Talking heads — dont worry about the Government
Melvins — forgotten Principles
Led Belly — ~~they~~ they Hung him on a cross
AC$DC — Soul Stripper
Rem — 190000
**PiL** — whatever
Lush — How does it feel to want
flipper — Shed No Tears ~~HAHAHA~~
Soundgarden — Heretic
Blue Oyster ~~Culture club~~ — kick out the Jams
Metallica — thing that should not be
Psychedellic ~~furs~~ Pistols — Pulse
Sexedellic furs — Bodies
S~~eptic furstols~~ — ~~Sister Europe~~ Soul Asylum — Aint that **Tough**
~~Bad Brains~~ — ~~Joshua's song~~ James Addiction — 1%
Necros — Blissard of Glass
Roy — in dreams
GREEN RIVER — OZZY
Aerosmith — Nobodys fault

# Bitching About PRog-Rock

Ing lots of Ings. Descriptive words
end IN INg. like masturbating, over exagerating
munching, chewing hot stacked-
earth momma sitting in the open woods of
Nottingham early in the mornings fog. listening
to stairway to Heaven while stringing beads. Not
applying makeup. In tune, Aqua man circles
emulating from a forehead. Bouncing off of a crystal
necklace. A neck strangled by piano wire.
"I have friends both on land and in the sky."
But the Sea mR French? "I dog paddle for I am
now a teeny little goblin-dancing-pixie-
-Zamphire master of the pan flute."

Sold over a zillion archery dummies in Europe
alone! The dummys are sex dolls stuffed with
leaches & a substance of Ginger Root, penny Royal
tea, Ginseng, B-vitamins, sweet cut-grass
and a spoiled pound of ground baby veal (lamb.)
Doctor Bronner claims! apply the archery
dummy-substance naked in the forest. Dilute!
Dilute! MR Merlin. Dilute! Dilute!
sprinkling minute metal shavings into the eyes of
a praised cult figure. A male.
Here now in the woods. Getting back to nature.
the breath is visible as he exhales from
the bull-like nostrils. scraping back leg
into the ground, mounting the earth momma.
no matter how hard you try, sex will always
Resurface.
Buffy and Jody get it on. Rick wakeman
does the soundtrack.

Hi   first of all I enjoy your show.

Jesse Helms is a dirty homosexual.
The Imperial wizard of the KKK is a nigger.
~~Such of thee harsh words of a sweet or sour~~
~~Bitter beer batter grease splatter scatter~~
~~Mad Hatter.~~
~~Do you like the show?~~
        Am I guilty of such hipness?
    NO longer is there hipness or such Tom foolery
for this boy whos name is ~~Cody~~. Hi that is my
name. I was thinking thee other day.
of my name and thought I would write you
NOT in regards to my name regardless of thee
sentence which may have thrown you off.
or ~~got you~~ off. I could only be such a
fool to modestly think ~~such as Lord could~~
~~think~~ How could one such suck winding-force
of so many celebs colons in hopes of
~~celebrating her~~ celebrating the calibre of
Such hipness. May I throw out my hip?
I had a bad fall. I limped.
I limped with the best of them.
    I have now come to the conclusion
that I have been ●● confused for many
days and I now love many days and
many many of those I love whom I have
So wrongly accused of being hip.
    Those who come to celebrate with one
Another only for the reasons of
companionship in which they so
Rightly share. They share the
same things. They seek out
    others. So fuck.
At peace am I. ~~Because~~        you're a good one.

"MONTE VISTA" SO TACOMA WAY

The name even reakes of
suburban subdivision Hell. I walked
into the place to buy a patch cord.
After I bought it I noticied a bunch
of amps behind a sliding glass door.
There were new Peavys marshalls
Fenders. After Gawking at the
list price I checked out the
used amps. I noticed an old
Fender. It's the kind thats about
fur feet tall and has SIX
tens in it. It's basically a twin
reverb. So I closed the door, plused
in the cheap Peavey tryout
gee-tar And fucked around with
the reverb & tremolo. It sounded
pretty cool kind of like the
cramps. SHit it was only $200.00,
It kind of beat, so I was
interested. Fuck it, I cranked it
up way loud to see what kind
of balls it had. Right then
mr. Suavo coolo Friedly
store dude walked in and turned
it down. He had a shit eating
grin on and said "Jams eE".
I said "Yeah man.

"Can I put this on Lay-a-way".
He said "Sure $20 bucks down
15 bucks a week for ninety
days". "Far out" He went away
so I cranked it again, so he
walks back in with his diaharaha
smile and turns it down.
What a dick I should have
thrown it threw the godamn
sliding glass door. I said
Sheeeatt! I left. That old
Fuckin fender would a blew any
way.

Globetrotters theme
Lucy in the Sky - William Shatner
The sensitive little boy - pro Gay Record
Pusherman - super fly sndtrk
Shes got you - Patsy Cline
frustrated - chipmunk punk (snack)
Keep yer hands off her - leadbelly
  JAVA - Floyd Cramer
  In love ⟩ Marine Girls
  **Honey**

mollys lips - Vaselines
**Ballad of Evel Knievel**
Somethin like that - NWA
TV Girl - Beat Happening
Scratch it out ⟩ Go team (Tam sings)
Bikini twilight⟩ me & Calvin & Toby
He never said a mumblin word - Leadbelly

Telly SAVALAS Greasing up his head And Ramming it
in And out! IN And out of Another TV personalities
ASS. whos ASS? who cares. either way its A
cheAp WAY to get An immediate lAugh.

← put the stars name here.

~~It could be even more Affective if~~ it is a male.
~~Homosexual scandals amongst celebrities are always a
shure fire chuckle getter.~~

OR ~~How About Goober And Gomer givin it to eachother.
Gary Coleman (Arnold on Different Strokes) and
emanuelle lewis (webster) versus monkey love in
the 69 tongue butt position.~~ WHY AM I
~~so sexually conscious? why can I not be
clean? Have I read too many porns? or charles
Bukowski?~~ Is this the easy WAY out?
NO. Sex is dirty. It is over rated.
"I dont want to be touched After its over."
"It wasnt worth it to cheat on my partner."
It took him 3 days to realize why he was
depressed. After All, his male friends
Approved with smurks And trumpeting farts.
Besides tellys stubble scratched the inner walls of
my colon. Do not be fooled by shiny,
WAXy baldness. His neck WAS A
JACK HAmmer. Very talented. shecky Greene
Joined in. We ran up A Huge gold cARd
Bill. Thats Alright, Im A High Roller.
All my celebrity friends are Here with me.
Here in LAs VegAs. NAked, shaved And Greased.
These lifesize cardboard cut-outs store AWAy eAsily in my
Closet. Lolli pop up you know where.
Lolli lolli lolli pop.

OH I'm so damn proud ~~of them~~. You ~~Oh another~~

A Triumphant victory for mandkind. Maybe there

is Hope. ~~Oooo ~~ It brought a tear to

& A lump in my throat

my eye. Staring out the window in a traffic jam

for 3 hours watching the little lawnmower cars zoom

past hundreds of happy westerners, receiving them

with a compassionate, full contact smile and stare.   You've

made it.   Have some fruit.   Now you too can purchase

pastel bed sheets, Electronics and toilet paper of

your ~~most~~ wildest dreams.   You have so much to learn.

Thousands of Grown infants, Rosy red cheeks ~~teeps~~

fully dressed in acid wash pants & jackets,

males with moustache, Ladies with permanent hair.

Look over there! it's my mom.      she ~~was~~ is

so many years more advanced in the art of shopping &

matching outfits from the luxury of selection.

You have so much to learn. Rock and Roll has

now just begun.     Don't hide the products

you have bought under your seats.    prepare yourself

for a full search as you enter back through the

border.    Take note of the leaflets and flyers

~~informed you~~ on your windshield informing you

where to acquire credit. And legal representation I'm happy for you.

please Reproduce.    we're doing all we can

over here as well.


groon

APly

APPly

Slowly carefully and righteously

walk you

through the

mysterious

world of

fashion

Laydown your warm babies on my cold feet
at the end of my bed ~~and then~~
I apologize ~~and~~ apologizing ~~red drink~~
~~the peeeeeered dive there the peter cooked~~
Taste ~~buds soak absorbent sponge~~ water and
my tongue runs across the roof of my mouth
and it feels like a small rib cage
                    Giant Nose Hair Booger Hinge

~~I~~ don't mind my captivity, but the pelt
~~and my~~ and habitat description ~~and be left~~
next to the cage is a bit ~~taste~~ distasteful.
Fucking Bull had a vision, He would write a
⊙ Punk Rock opera

## THE STORY

His name is forest and he is the one
who put's calcium in the Tab soft drinks.
and his followers wave their arms in unison
with ~~him~~ his. Clenching crimping irons and
mascara (black), "We must make the woods
Pretty again"), shouted the steam engine inventor.
    Yes but what about the piles of masses?
the Heaping mounds of sponge, severed Pore,
and Taste bud chunks, nervously bitten and
spat out of the mouth from the Chiwawa
Head, Johnny Mathis monster? asked chowder.)
    It is sucking dry all the resin from the
Bong Water River. I say we destroy the filter
walls.' (shouted Helium Boy.) And then (fucking) spoke..
                                            (Bull)

Skip 2 Pages
And GO ON ⟶

He SPAT ~~Out~~ Dark brown bubbling snoose from
the dried veins of New Age believers. it soaked
into the ground instantly which reminded him
~~that~~ the woods are in greater need of emergency
than he thought. he said "look my friends,
spit and see the quickness of the soil.
      And as all 5 beings spat and observed.
Tony Defranco crabs surfaced and gobbled
what little moisture they could before being
stepped on and crushed and quickly ~~gobbled~~ consumed
~~up~~ by our hero's. the feast was celebrated
with an offering of ~~spam~~ fresh squeezed
grease pockets of spam and pepperoni
chunks filled to the rim of an ancient
1990's ~~~~ teenage unwanted baby skull.
      But this does not explain our misfortune
Grunted Buttchowder. Please, please tell
us more Fucking Bull and so Fucking Bull spoke again.
      It was in my. vision that I saw stoners
destroy a church with no roof and only 3
walls. And there were candles, many candles
And the Virgin Mary Hooked ~~on~~ thru
her back on a meat Hook, and one of
the male stoners said "Dude Hooker headers."
then stopped dead in his tracks with his
hand just softly touching her firm breast
and noticed how painfully Beautiful she was,
how pure. and white, how peaceful wrapped
in chicken and barbed wire with not yet

ON All drums - get rid of Hi HAT Hiss.

_Downer_ - Re-Do All vocals & get someone with A
Deep Voice to repeat solo vocals in monotone
~~Dub~~ Re-Do All Guitar & bass

_floyd_ - Re-Do bass - Dub extra Guitar

_Paper Cuts_ - Dub Guitar - Dub Singing Harmony
~~Dub~~ Re-Do·Bass

_Spank thru_ - Re-Do Bass

~~Love Buzz~~

_Hairspray Queen_ - Re-Do everything

_Pen Cap chew_ - Re·Do everything

_Mexican Seafood_ = Re-Do Guitar Drums Voc.
         (Dales drums)
ERECTUM

Love Buzz  Bigcheese  ERECTUM  weirdo
BeesWAX  Aeroszeppelin  VendetAGainst
ANNoveYorcist

A finished Anarchy sign spray painted on her Robe. Then his head turned slowly to his mates, ~~And cried~~ A trickle of Teardrop Rolled down his ugly fucking zitted out face And cried: "This is WRONG! We MUST STOP This!"

and so One of the girl stoners kind of put All her weight on one foot And stuck her Acid wash ASS out, ~~hold A cigarette~~ took A big drag off of A lucky STRike cigarette, gave a very cool blank/stoned expression under those heavily eye shadow (Blue) thicker than snot lashed eyes, exhaled And in A groggy dry wheezing, charred lung voice said, "so whAT were bored." And the others immediately Ran Around screaming, wooo Hooo (in that tone of voice that says "I'm Very drunk, excited And A Total idiot") they smashed And Burned And SPRAYed Black, flag, DR ~~⊗~~ as well as Dokken And Whitesnake. Then Guess whaT? Asked fucking Bull, ~~they added A shite they got~~ Bored ~~and went away~~ WHAT? WhAT happened shit Butt chowder? fucking Bull said: ~~th~~ After Awhile they became bored with vandalizing the church And went ~~⊗~~ Away to buy A GRAM. So I suggest we All just connect our vitals to this ancient cow milking HookAH And Relax, because the River will never dry up for it is fed by the mountains which will ALWAYS be Addicted to boredom.

The END

83

Fear - We gotta get outta this place
Gary Numan - It must have been years
PIL - Annalisa
Elvis Costello - Pump it up
Pop o pies - I am the walrus
Tales of Terror - Chambers of Horror

BRing

SNARE

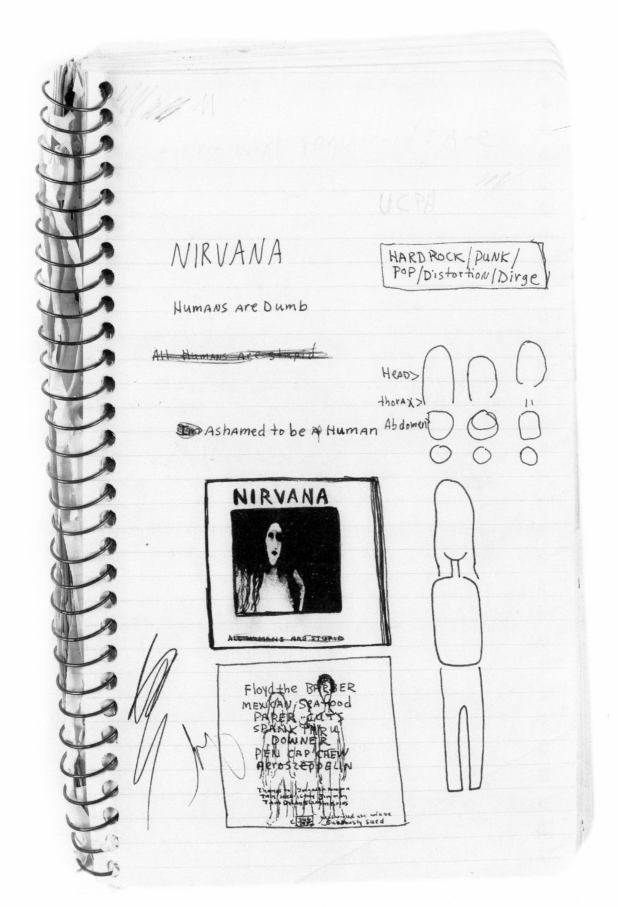

NIRVANA

HARD ROCK / PUNK /
POP / Distortion / Dirge

Humans are Dumb

~~All Humans are stupid~~

I'm Ashamed to be a Human

NIRVANA

ALL HUMANS ARE STUPID

Head >
thorax >
Abdomen

Floyd the BARBER
MEXICAN SEAFOOD
PAPER CUTS
SPANK THRU
DOWNER
PEN CAP CHEW
AEROZEPPELIN

# Critic goes GOD

The first thing i did WAS burn All my Charles Bukowski books. I got the tinfoil out and spread it on the floor, Ripped the ~~books~~ filthy innards of plankton-literature into small pieces, and struck A match. I Turned out the lights And watched the flames Along with some home Super 8 movies I had made while under the influence of this life I've decided to change. The movies were typical Gore slash shit Along with puppets fucking, oh And the psychic TV-~~rainbow~~-like effect of ArTy subjects turning And floating ~~about~~ in a meaningful surrealistic sense. bullshit, it WAS like watching A Real estate seminar, but it set A nice background for my MTV Direction towards god. God. God. God. I'm crosslegged, Rosary to ~~my Right, Bible to my left.~~ the left of me, Bible to the Right, here I Am stuck in the middle with you". stuck in the middle with you.' Who Sang that song? Atlanta Rhythm Section? Steve miller, Um, God. 'Atlanta Rhythm Section hAs the dorkiest looking members, that one Guy with Greasy pig fat hAir, And Black Rimmed Glasses. But the

Stupidest looking 70's Rock star has to
be that one guy in SLADE, the fucker
cut his bangs so high up on his forehead.
"He looks like Woody from the bay City
Rollers". I know this kid in Aberdeen
who looks EXACTLY like Woody. Jesus you
wouldn't believe it, the same teeth and
Nose, ~~it's note sad it's just funny~~.
I would love to look like Woody, then
I could start my band and keep play
Saturday Night. "WAS kiss on
Saturday Night live? NAW ~~they~~ they
couldn't have, ~~fans~~ would have trashed
the studio & beat up Don PARDO, ~~and
Raped Lorraine Newman.~~ I would love
to be those kids on the back of Kiss
Alive, the ones holding the banner.
Kiss. I don't even like kiss.
    Rock Trivia. God im so sick
of Rock Trivia, big deal it's like
what am i gonna do when Im old,
if i already know everything about
Rock-n-Roll by the time im 19?
    God only knows ~~actually~~ there's
No facts to be learned about all these
worthless Ripoff Nostalgic bands. of the 80's
    Oh yeah i decided to eventually
become an H Addict and slowly decay
on the streets of Idaho. or some

middle of the road ▓▓ state like that.
I'll be so bored that ill just read
About what I lived thru And purposely
stayed NAive, because you mR Rock
Critic Are gonna be Bored when your old.
Bored Bored Bored. So Am I so Are
old people today, I don't wANt A
GrAnd dAughter of mine chAnging my soiled
Rubber underwear And sucking on Ry-Krisp,
while F
clinging to existence just so I cAn
reminice About my life As A professional
Remeniscent. Besides, my memory
is AlreAdy shot, from too much PoT
smoking A few yeArs back. I saw
these Hippies on the merve Griffin show
claiming they had NASAl SPRAys wich
would increAse you're memory, I Also
SAw this couple who swore, with the
proper trAining, "you cAn hAve up to 10
orgAsms before ejAculAting, sure
if you tie A rubber bAnd to the end.
       All this wonderfully importAnt
deep thought hindered me from REAlizing
that the entire House WAS filled
with smoke from the chArles Bukowski
Books, And A very nice sized flAme
had spreAd to the curtAins, which AlArmed
me I had only A few minutes to
Get out of the House, so much for God.

Sexually Transmitted Diseases
in the espresso At the Smithfield

Green River — Aint Nothin to do
Dead Boys — Dead River Boys
Dicks — Police force
Clown Alley — on the way up
Vox Pop — Production
**SKIN DIVER** — αD No. 7
Shock'n Blue — HoT SAND
Bangles — HAzy Shade of Winter
the eyes — Dont talk to me
Saccharine Trust — Peace frog
~~Youre N~~ Big Dipper — Youre NoT Patsy
Big BLACK — CRACK UP
Big Boys — A Political
Alice Cooper — Muscle of Love
GRey Sage — StRAight AHEAD
MAlfunkshuN — Stars And YOU
**SMelvins** —
           Smell My Finger
DeVO — TURN AROUND

White Zombie — RaTmouth
Zombies — Time of the SEASON
**DicKs** — off Duty SAilor
A PART of the Tape that will be fast forwarded every time it's played
The Tonsil Song — HA HA HA HA HA HA HA HAHA

Throughout the periods of 1976 to 1983, a man by the name of Chuck Taylor brutally sexually Tortured 9 women, one man and one 13 yr old boy, within the area of Greater Los Angeles.

In Comparison to other so called "Celebrity" murderers one wouldn't think if Chuck's case as a Record setting toll of victims, in mathematical sense, (no". yet in Ritualistic Highly detailed, well planned task for the bizarre (yes". Chucks story hasn't become the most well know folk tale as had ED Geine, simply because facts haven't been revealed as in depth until now, where ED Geine may have wore his victims skin and ate their flesh, Chuck did that and far exceeded Ed's descriptiveness for his own so called Ceremony. Chuck recorded every day of his waking life.

suicide note found with chuck Taylors body feb. 17. 1983

To whom it may concern,

Please excuse Chucks absence from life. I ~~cant~~ I do not expect anyones sorrow for my death maybe relief if anything. I cant describe what mental illness is. Ive tried and tried with writings and doctors and my only conclusion is satan has taken over my soul and mind, please use my brain as an example and try to find out whats wrong, like the guy in texas who shot those people in the tower. to all the relatives & friends of my victims Im deeply sorry I'm very sorry. Ha HA HA Im not sorry HA HA HAHA HA You mother fuckers Cunt! Chuck Taylor,
not A basketball star.

Born Sept 1st 1958 in Santa Clara California
Chuck Joseph Taylor, son of Fred and Mary Taylor was a perfectly normal
Healthy, Happy baby, full of sunshine and Joy.
A first Grandson and nephew for both sides of the
family, Chuck was the center of attention, often hearing
harmless quarrels over "who gets to hold him" between
several young teenage Aunts.                    Fred and Mary
just married out of Highschool, were immature, just
starting out, already used to their white trash homestyle.
Depression hadn't set in yet so they were pretty much Happy.
Fred had a short temper and worked two jobs
while mary with another baby on the way stayed at home
giving young chuck now 5 yrs old more than enough loving
attention and encouragement.              He loved monsters. All
kinds, they were more interesting than super heroes and often
against his parents wishes he would plead with his baby
sitter to let him watch the friday night Horror movies,
and very consistently would end up crying or wetting
his pajamas in fear within minutes of the beginning.
Yet he still insisted, "monsters are the best"
he had drawings, comic books, posters, models and masks
Truly an obsession, but most of his influences were
cheesy old space invader or Dracula movies. wich has
baffled doctors on his case of wich, why or how he
possibly could think up such vulgar re-enactments of
horror while playing with his sisters dolls. arranging
nativity scenes of murder with Jesus mary and Joseph
figurines along with, G-I joes and barbie's, cautiously
cutting holes in them filling them up with moms red
nail polish. finding him in a trance like state rocking back
and forth screaming fuck you bad peoples Fuck you

He was usually very clean about his seizures, He
always made sure there were newspapers down and a
wash rag handy And the knives and matches were on an
old cigar box the lights dim, curtains closed, wearing the
same old football jersey that was way too small, no pants
And most important to make sure dad wasn't home.
        Recalling many painful instances his younger
sister Jenny was often unable to defend for herself Against
Chucks agressive abuse, he was always holding her down
~~him~~ and sat on her ~~lap~~ face and farting, talking her into
A ~~tasting~~ guessing game, tied to a chair and blindfolded tickled
till she peed her pants and then forced to taste a
collected sample and regularly sexually explored her,
    "He wouldn't do the usual tortures like other older
brothers, like a simple peeled grape and being told its
A cats eyeball, Chuck would always give me tobasco sauce
or his soiled finger that had been up his Anus, call it
relative blood or whatever I still ~~can't~~ couldn't help but feel
sorry for him, because he's the one that witnessed
dad's abuse towards mom."
        Almost every night Fred Taylor came
home from a degrading laymens job intoxicated,
hungry and very angry.    as if it were a routine
at 7:30 each nite chuck would be greeted by
his dad standing in ~~the~~ his bedroom doorway
swaying back and forth with a transfixed hateful
expression. "Git in here boah its time to see how
bad yer momma's been today, come on Goddamnit!
Git yer fucking little wimpy ass in here! grabbing
him by the neck chuck would be pushed into
his parents bedroom, the door slamming shut
and mom already naked huddled on a

corner of the bed in a natural crying plead knowing that she might as well get it over with before dinner gets too cold.    Taking off his belt, loosening his trousers fred would beat mary Rape and Sodomize her ~~just hard enough to be classified as S/M~~ during the intercourse chuck was commanded to watch while fred stared at his son and Repeated the same speech every night.   your Gonna grow up to be a man chucky A man! you see this winch? theyre good for nothin but cookin and fuckin! your Gonna go to school and yer gonna be a doctor chuck Goddamnit your not gonna be like me you hear? ugly A good Boy that's my Boy you fuckin Bitch! ugly! ugly turning to mary you had to have kids, well these kids is gonna be fine, people not Bad like you ugly fucking Bitch! Chucky? what you gonna do Boah? A winner I cant hear you! a winner dad ok now go on Git.    Jenny was never asked to witness this probably because dad thought when she gets older she could leech off of a rich Boy and support ~~~~ Daddy and momma

Chuck would never talk about it when I questioned him i felt so sorry for him that i must have felt this self destructive need to Put up with his abuse and chuck had a very clever and sly way of mixing laughing Playing and having fun with abuse.. one minute ~~~~ we would be playing & the next he would Hit me and go into a Jekyll and Hyde personality, then when his tension was relieved he would comfort me to stop my crying begging me not to tell mom and Hell never do it again. Bribes of candy or Toys were ALWAYS a good pay off for a 4 yr old little Girl, and if bribes didn't work threats' usually would.

With good intentions and noticing traces of Abnormal hyperactive behavior and numerous complaints from school Mary Taylor devoted A lot of time in helping Chuck become more relaxed. after All if "VAlium helped her nerves, then why not chucks!) the long talks and reading time special Attention seemed to help some, but the long term affect of downers seemed to counteract to his nerves A bit too strong, wich bore the many trips to the doctors for Treatment of hypertension and involuntary nervous seizures, chuck now 9 yrs old by this time is very used to medications.

School was fine in kindergarten, he seemed to have A few good friends and willing to learn gave him the everpopular standard mark by his teacher as "A pleasure to have in class" but gradually thru 1st And second grader chucks over bearing personality gave him quite A few enemies especially with girls, the pretty ones were afraid of him and the ugly ones got beat up by him. Condemning unatractive people At such an early age proved to be A key relation to his antics later on in life. As a few psychologists on chucks case Agreed it started when chuck now proclaimed "A future responsible man" by his father was asked to dispose of A retarded kitten one of seven wich eventually dissapeared all in A litter of his sisters momma cat sno white. A Gunny sack in the river was expected not cutting of decappatation, cutting it's stomach out, spreading the innards on his face And Repeatedly running his tongue on its rib cage. when Questioned of this by one of the psychologists chuck Replied

"I wanted to see if the roof of my mouth felt the same as a rib cage, and you know what? it does! everybody ~~has~~ in the world has rib cages in the roof of their mouths - cool huh? He also insisted that peas have mashed potatoes in them". His mother remembers. "He seemed to have a different pet each month it wasn't until ~~years~~ after he moved out that we found all the animal bones in the basement."

Over looking his serious hyperactivity kids ~~people~~ that knew him couldn't help but admit that Chuck had a very bizarre yet funny sense of humor, this humor crowned him the class cut up and falsely gave him friends who took advantage of him just to see the next gag which was always directed ~~towards~~ hurting, scaring or humiliating an individual, and by the 6th grade at age 12 he experienced his first expell from school by defacating in a paper towel and hurling it into the face of an unpopular teacher. and when he was let back to school it was well worth it for he had even more attention from his peers.

ELVIS
Cooper

# Aneurysm

Come on over & do the twist

over do it & have a fit

Come on over & shoot the shit

I love you so much it makes me
sick

she keeps it pumpin straight to my heart

# SAPPY

And if you save yourself
you will - think your happy
Hell keep you in a Jar
then youll - think your happy
Hell give you breather Holes
then youll - think your happy
Hell cover you in grass
then youll - think your happy now

(Your in a (aundry Room)
Conclusion came to you AM


And if you HEAL yourself
you will make Him happy
youll wallow in your shit


And if you cure yourself

# Verse Chorus Verse

Neither side is sacred ~~there's no room~~ no one wants to win
feeling so sedated think I'll just give in
TAKin medication till our stomachs full
wouldn't wanna fake it - if I hAd A soul

The grass is greener over here
your the fog that keeps me clear
your the REASon I Feel PAIN

~~feels so good to feel Again~~ (scribbled out)

feels so good to feel Again
hAve to wonder why Im green
I have to pure YoA out of me

Imodium H
Lithium SH
Dive H
Polly S
SAPPY P
token EAstern song H
Verse chorus verse P
IN Bloom H
PAY to PLAY H
~~Not like them~~ S I think im dumb
Been A son P

MAybe when Im younger I'll refuse to Grow
injecting ~~Nutrition~~ progress moves too slow
maybe when im older ~~stomach in~~
MAybe when ~~IM~~ ready we could try Again

# Dive

Pick me - Pick me YEAH
Let a low long Signal
At ease   At least yeAH
everyone is Hollow
Pick me — Pick me yeAH
everyone is wAiting
Pick me - Pick me yeAH
~~You will~~ even pay them
You cAn
    Hey
   Dive Dive Dive Dive in me

Kiss this kiss that yeAH
let a low long Signal
At ease AtEAse yEAH
You cAn be my Hero
Pick me pick me yeAH
everyone is ~~wAiting~~ ~~Hollow~~ wAiting
Hit me  Hit me yeah
~~Recor even SwAllow~~
I'm reAl good At HAting

101

Hi Eugene,

I'm staying at a friends house here in Olympia listening to a crappy college radio show. I've realized that it's not because there are no good bands but because the DJ's have Bloody awful taste in music. OH yes, and to prove my point, right now theyre playing a ~~████~~ NIRVANA song from an old Demo.

How's Captain America? I hear were playing some shows together when we go over to England. I can't wait! were really looking forward to it. all our friends will be there at Redding. mudhoney Baterin Toytoy Sonic Youth, ~~Dggyetc~~Ashure blow out!

well, we won the WAR.

Patriotic propaganda is in fulleffect.

We have the privilege of purchasing Desert Storm trading cards, flags, bumperstic and many video versions of our triumphant victory, When I walk down the street I feel like I'm at a ~~█~~ Nurenburg rally.

Hey, maybe Nirvana & Captain America could go on tour together in the states and burn American flags on stage. well be going out again in Sept If youre interested, I'll keep you posted. well, heres the live mollys lips 7" I find it embarrasing because it's just simply a bad version but it was a great privilege to play one of your songs and to play together at a show and to meet you all. It was easily the "GREATEST MOMENT OF MY LIfe"

The Vaselines have been my favorite # 1
band for a long while now and and
Geez. I can't wait to see you all
soon and thanks for writing.

    andy(jim's) I got evicted from my apt. I am living in
my car so I have no address but here's
            chris's phone number for messages

        your pal kurdt

Derek

1   Stooges — Raw power
2   Beatles — ~~meet the Beatles~~ Something new
3.  Leadbellys last sessions
4   Scratch Acid — 1st EP
5.  Butthole surfers — 1st EP
6.  Vaselines — 1st EP
7.  Fang — Land Shark
8   Smithereens — especially for you
9   Tales of terror — tales of terror
10. Pixies — Surfer Rosa
11. mudhoney — super fuzz Bigmuff
12. Flipper — Generic flipper
13. Black flag — my war
14. Black Sabbath — master of Reality
15. credence Clearwater — Bayou
16. Blue cheer — Vincebus eruptum
17. The Knack — Get the Knack
18. Saccharin trust — 1st EP
19. Roy Orbison — greatest hits
20  Gang of four — Entertainment
21. Wipers — ~~Youth of America~~ is this real
22. Shocking Blue — shocking Blue
23. Bad brains — Rock for light
24. Best Happening — Jamboree
25. Aerosmith — Rocks
26. Shonen Knife — is cassette burning farm
27. young marble Giants — ymG
28. velvet underground — white light white heat
29. Sex pistols — never mind the Bullocks

Disclaimer

- ☐   I am threatened by ridicule
- ☐   I am overly concience of ~~so~~ the sincerity in my voice.
- ☐   I like to have sex with ~~so~~ people
- ☐   I love my parents yet I disagree with merely everything they stand for.
- ☐   I understand and appreciate the ~~value of~~ religion for ~~some people~~ others.
- ☐   my emotions are affected by music.
-        punk rock means freedom
- ☐   I use bits and pieces of others personalities to form my own.
- ☐
- ☐
- ☐

Hi, I like punk rock more than anything in the whole wide world. and so I thought I'dwould xerox words on paper & staple them together and sell them to punk Rockers & others who don't know much about Punk Rock and for those who dont care or who dont deserve the privilege and also to those who are Bored with it.

I Also dont know very much About PUNK Rock

AS far As the History is concerned Well, me too. I'm bored ~ or just uninspired. maybe were just taking a break, a rest or But I recovery from Hardcore. I never do really liked hardcore, mainly because I HAVE it was too macho and there were AN so many intimidating rules. I remember OPINION when I first started hanging out with friends of ON who were a few months more advanced in WHAT proper punk rock lingo & etiquette, I PUNK said, "hey lets listen to some punk," and ROCK this guy said "man its not called means punk anymore its called HARD CORE! to Gee, I felt like a heel. HARD CORE me was an obvious mutation of 77 punk it means because punk popularity reached the freedom suburbs and then all of a sudden jocks from: who already had short hair from the wrestling team got involved because it was supposedly an easy energy release and an excuse to fight. I could probably explain why I never liked hardcore in a million different ways but lets just say it wasn't my cup of TEA, All you have to do is read the letter section from MAXIMUM Rock-n-Roll from the past 6 years and you may understand what I mean.

Dispensable as recycled toilet tissue, they breed like rabbits and their hands will be sent back attached to key chains. If Jimmi Hendrix were alive he would more than likely have a long back (bi level) hair cut and slick, sequin threads sporting a new Aero dynamic-90's guitar with zebra stripes and a pointy headstock. Iggy pop at a recent gig in L.A. jammed with slash from Guns-n-roses on a 20 minute rendition of louie louie.

The journalist left a red ~~circle~~ circle, imprint from the camera lens on the forehead of a mother who has 5 sons in the persian gulf. She was asked to describe just exactly how she feels of this situation while holding her sons ~~her son's~~ military portraits in her lap. A student listening to old R.E.M watches the mother on T.V. and becomes exited by the idea that has just burst from his environmentally & sicially ~~conscious~~ mind: "maybe there will be reason now for A REVOLUTION!

I like following the rise of entertainers careers while they still ~~haven't to~~ maKe it, ~~while in their early to late twenties~~. I like to know everything about them, and if enough information isn't available, then tabloids will be sufficient. I like punk rock. I like girls with weird eyes. I like drugs. I like passion. I like things that are built well. I like innocence. I like and am grateful for the blue collar worker whos existence allows Artists to not have to work at ~~menial~~ jobs. I like killing gluttony. I like playing my cards wrong.

But my Body And mind won't Allow me to TAKE them

I like various styles of music. I like making
fun of musicians whom I feel pladgerise or
offend music as art by exploiting/pushing their
embarrasingly, pathetic versions of their work.
I like to write poetry. I like to ignore others onto
poetry. I like vinyl. I like nature and animals.
I like to swim. I like to be with my friends.
I like to be by myself. I like to feel guilty
for being a white, American male.
   I love to sleep. I like to fill my mouth
with seeds and spit them out at random
as I walk. I like to taunt small, barking
dogs in parked cars. I like to make people feel
happy and superior in their reaction towards
my appearance. I like to feel predjudice
 towards people who are predjudice. I like
to make incisions into the belly of infants then
fuck the incisions until the child dies.
   I like to dream that someday we will have
a sense of Generational Solidarity amongst the
youth of the world. I like to make insidious
efforts to Avoid Conflict. I like to have
strong opinions with nothing to back them up
with besides MY PRIMAL sincerity.
      I like sincerity. I LACK sincerity.
these are not opinions. these are not words of wisdom.
this is a disclaimer, a disclaimer for my
lack of education, for my loss of inspiration,
for my unnerving Quest for affection and
my perfunctory shamefullnes of towards many who
are of my relative age. Its not even A
Poem. its Just A Big pile of shit. like ME.

I like to complain and do nothing to make things better. I like to blame my parents generation for coming so close to social ~~equal~~ change then giving up after a few successful ~~efforts~~ by the media & Government ~~to~~ deface the movement by ~~using~~ using the mansons ~~as~~ and other Hippie representatives as ~~examples~~ propaganda examples on how they were nothing but unpatriotic, communist, satanic, unhuman diseases. And in turn the baby boomers become the ultimate, conforming, yuppie hypocrites a generation has ever produced.

I like to calmly and rationally discuss my views in a conformist manor even though I consider myself to the extreme left.
I like to infiltrate the mechanics of a system by posing as one of them, then slowly start the rot from the inside of the empire.
I like to ~~assassinate~~ the lesser & greater of two evils.
I like to impeach God.
I like to Abort christ.
I like to fuck sheep.
I like the comfort in knowing that women are ~~Generally~~ superior, ~~and~~ and naturally less violent than men.
I like the comfort in knowing that women are the only future in rock and roll.

I like the comfort in knowing that the
Afro American invented Rock and roll
yet has only been rewarded, or awarded
for their accomplishments when conforming
to the white mans standards.
   I like the comfort in knowing that the
Afro American has once again been the
only race that has brought a new form
of original music to this decade! hip hop/rap.

## censorship is VERY American.

   I have met many minds able to store and translate
a pregnantly large amount of information, yet
they havent an ounce of talent for wisdom or
the appreciation Of passion.

   The conspiracy towards success in America (unamericuh)
is immediacy. To expose in great repetition to the minds of
small attention spans. fast, speedy, now with even more
nacho cheese flavor! here today, gone tomorrow because
yesterdays following was nothing more than a tool in every
individuals need for self importance, entertainment and
social rituals. Art that has long lasting value cannot
be appreciated by majorities, only the
same, small percent will value Arts patience
as they always have. this is good. the ones
who are unaware do not deserve false suggestions
in their purchasing duties.

tips

III

~~music has nothing~~ ~~nothing~~ to do with a
~~musicians personal beliefs, its not an~~ extention
of ~~personality~~ ~~a story~~ ~~surface~~ ~~minds of~~
~~feelings~~
scenarios revolve. verbal communication is
exhausted. sit coms are scenarios and so
is our conversation. ~~to gather~~
~~for a party to gather to~~

out of
our party gathers ~~to congregate~~ boredom.
role playing for affection & acceptance and
to disinfect nagging germs ending in silence,
and accomplishment-produced violations
on those who werent here to play.
  they were invited, maybe in a museum
far from now.
I Am now ~~sad~~ in my sad stage, before it
was naive hate. I want to be the first
to discover and discard before its
popularity. Tomorrow the I wont care
stage is predicted, and im not looking
forward to it. maybe vegetables will
diffuse the chemicals ~~which I produce~~.
i produce inside me. an easy excuse,
(these chemicals.) I rarely ~~ever~~ use
my instrument. it used to be so exciting.
working on music is not a chore. Its Now
a waste of time to practice. Every
other month I buy the results from
the Air.
Ask not what you can do to your rock stAr.

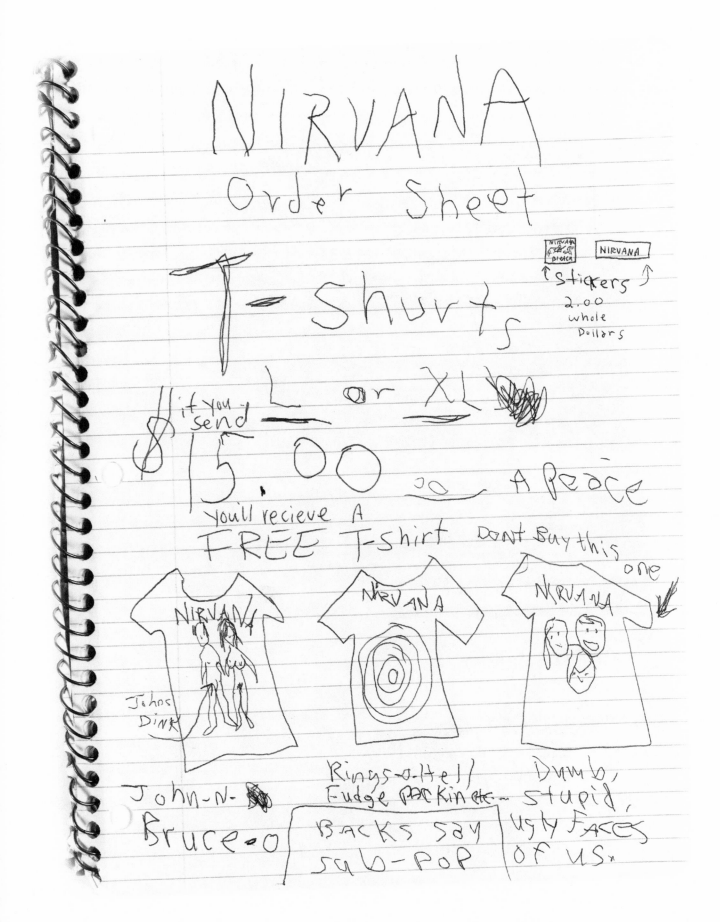

NIRVANA

Order Sheet

T-shurts

stickers
2.00
whole
Dollars

$ if you send L or XL

$15.00 ∞ A Peace

you'll recieve A
FREE T-shirt DON'T BUY this one

NIRVANA
Johns
DINK

NIRVANA

NIRVANA

John-N-
Bruce-o

Rings-o-Hell
Fudge packin etc
BACKS say
sub-pop

Dumb,
stupid,
ugly FACES
of us.

~~scribble~~

A manic depressive on smack floating in A WARM
deprevAtion tank, singing leonard cohen,
masturbating, watching golfers fish while
dreAming of A stamp collection.
~~scribble~~

the king of words is: EVERYthing

I can only fuck and **sing**.
HAve you ever felt like you cared so much that you
wanted to kill ~~scribble~~ your Germs?

who will be the king and queen of the outcasts?

I've lost my **MIND** many times, and my
wallet many more.
IN the simplest terms :
~~scribble~~

1  Dont RAPe
2  Dont be predjudice
3  Dont be Sexist
~~scribble~~
4  Love your children
5  Love your Neighbor
6  Love yourself
   Don't let your opinions  obstruct
     the Aforementioned list

114

I was about 13 and going through the common ~~you are puberty~~ pre-pubescent, hate your parents, wish you could still play with dolls but instead, feel unusually weird around girls-syndrome.

I was a rodent-like, underdeveloped, hyperactive spaz who could fit his entire torso in one leg of his bell bottomed jeans, and I was frustrated. I needed to let off some steam. I went to the movies with my friends. We saw "Over the Edge."

Over the edge is a ~~movie~~ story of troubled youth, vandalism, parental negligence, and most importantly ~~love~~ real estate development dysfunctional families

Its true in A sense that you can make A comfortable living At it ~~but other than~~ ~~that is not~~ ~~a profession too~~ A prof in of A profession. But besides financial security it really isnt that wise of a profession. one of the main problems i have ~~because~~ I feel like im being evaluated is that 24 hrs A day, ~~being in a band~~ is hard work and the acclaim itself ~~just~~ isnt worth it unless you still like playing And I do god how I do love playing live, its the most primal form of energy release you can share with other people besides having sex or taking drugs. So if you see A good live show on drugs and then later that evening have sex, youve basically covered All the bases of energy release, and we All need to let off steam, its easier and safer than protesting Abortion clinics ~~or~~ praising God or wanting to hurt your Brother

so go to A
show dance around A Bit
and copulate

117

# Primary

The second time we broke it off
I ~~lost~~ a voice sincerity was washed
I love myself better than you - I know its
wrong so what should I do?

Im on a plaine - I cant complain

The 18th time we broke it off
I heard a noise ~~so~~ we burnt a cross
we walked hand in hand in our parade
~~we~~ took off our robes and began ~~to~~ rape


you stole things from me - All Apologies
I stole things from you - I will stand accused
what else can i do - I belong to you
what else can there be - All Apologies


what else can I say - All my words are grey
what else should I write? - I dont want to fight
how else could I feel? - All our lips are sealed
what do you expect? - Im a nervous wreck

in the sun in the sun i feel as one
in the sun in the SUN Im married
marriage
YEAH YEAH YEAH YEAH

# NOT Finished

## I Think I'm Dumb

mollys lips Slushy-VAselines

I'm not like them - but I can pretend
the sun is Gone - but I have A light
the day is done - but im having fun
I think im dumb - or maybe just happy

my heart is broke  but I have some Glue
Help me inhale & mend it with you
well float Around & hang out on clouds
then well come down & have a hangover.

Skin the sun & fall Asleep
breathe AWAY - the soul ~~~~ is weak
lesson learned - ~~~~ wish me luck
Soothe the burn - WAKE me up

I've been told that an artist is in need of constant tragedy to fully express their work, but I'm not an artist and when I say I in a song, that doesnt neccesarily mean that that ~~this~~ person is me and it doesn't mean im just a story teller, it means whoever or whatever you want because everyone has their own definition of specific words and when your dealing in the context of music you cant expect ~~universal meanings~~ words * to ~~have~~ the same ~~a~~ meaning as ~~in~~ everyday use of our vocabulary because I consider music art and when I say "that song is art," I dont mean in comparison to A painting because ~~If~~ the visual arts are not nearly as sacred as the transcribed or Audio Communications, but it is art and ~~there~~ ~~our was a more tragic loss like~~ somewhere ~~then the~~ I feel this society ~~and other~~ has lost it's ~~most~~ valuable sense of what art is, Art is expression. in expression you need 100% full freedom and our freedom to express our Art is seriously being fucked with. FUCK, the word fuck has as many connotations as does the word Art and ~~Im~~ ~~cot~~ far beyond the point of sitting down and casually ~~complaining~~ ~~exposing~~ this problem to the Right wing control freaks who Are the main ~~offenders~~ of destroying

Art. I ~~won't~~ wont calmly and Literally complain to ~~YOU~~! I'm going to fucking Kill. I'm going to fucking Destroy your MACHO, Sadistic, Sick Right wing, religiously Abusive opinions on how we As A whole should operate According to YOUR conditions. before I die many will die with me and they will deserve it. see you IN Hell
love kurdt
                                        cobain

      thanks for the TRAgedy I need
      it for my Art.
punk Rock is Art ~~the problem~~
  Punk Rock to me means freedom.
  the only problem i've had with the situationists
~~a~~ punk rock ~~ethic~~ is that Absolute denial
~~of~~ Anything ~~is~~ sacred, I find a ~~lot~~
few ~~of~~ things sacred ~~the~~ such as
the superior~~ity~~ ~~of~~ women and the negro
~~have~~ ~~and the things they've HAD to~~ Contribut~~ion~~
to ~~it~~ Art. I guess what im Saying is
that Art is sacred.
      punk rock is freedom
  expression And right to express is vital
Anyone CAN be artistic.

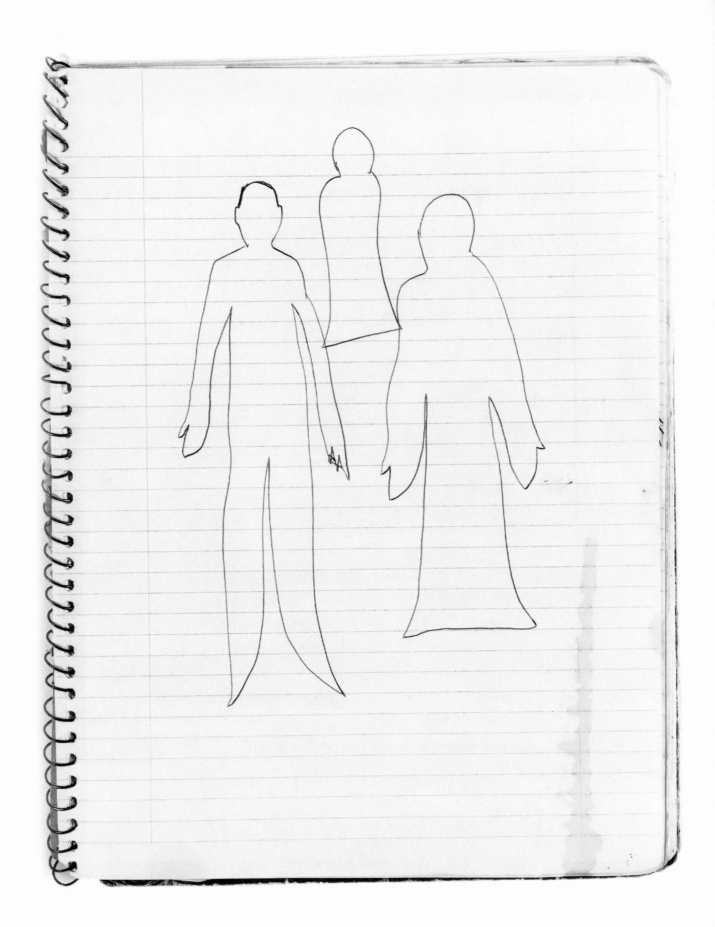

I have a lot to say, but ill leave that to
you, I'll leave that to those who have
the ability to expound better than I.
their whinies
The facts to back up the complaints
and the patience to debate, the
impossible deprogramming of the plantation
owners, and their workers and their slaves.
The slaves born into their world
UN-questioning, unaware through their
generationsacceptance of "thats just the
way it is", stripped of culture in
the pen, bred in a pen and losing
ink, but refilling pray of disposable
goods and pray of the dispensable through
the faith given by the feudal Lords "take it or leave it."
impulse "like it or lump it." "I brought you into this
world and ill take you out." "I'll be the judge
of that." No instinct to escape, crawling
over eachother in an overly populated
tank, just lying there waiting to be fed
eating more than you need and wanting
more cause you never know if its
ever going to come again. Breeding
& eating & waiting & complaining &
praying,

Starting from the arm pit of an old man, ~~and down~~
in a rush of slow motion - flood gates,
blown Wide-open,  sweat ~~like~~ butter melts downward
through the valleys of ripe, pink-prune skin,
wrapped loosely around his ~~marble~~ arm,
congregating at the tips of uncut, Brittle
Jaundiced fingernails,   beads meet and
~~Breed~~ ~~mix~~, then jump to their death,
they land as ~~splach~~ A splash on smoothe thighs
of infants lying limp on beds of ~~angels hair~~ mo-hair
dirty books made him solidify into a pedophile
Coalate Corelate
Corralate Coralate  Solidiphile into A Pedfile
Corilate
I'm not well read,  but when I do
read, I read well.
~~XXXXXXXXXX~~
I dont have the time to translate
what I understand in the form of conversation,
I had exhausted most conversation ~~this~~ at age nine.
I only feel with grunts screams and tones and with
hand gestures and my body. ~~and tones~~ im deaf in spirit.

~~I keep myself~~

I purposely keep myself naive  and away from
earthly information because its the only
way to avoid a jaded attitude.
      everything i do is ~~internally and~~ subronciousse
because you cant rationalize spirituality
      we dont deserve this privilege ~~⊘~~
      ~~I can only feel.~~
            I cant ~~████~~ or speak, I can only feel.
      maybe someday Ill ~~will~~ turn myself into
      Hellen Keller  by puncturing my ears
      with a knife, then cutting my voice box
            out.


      If you want to know what I ~~feel like~~
      the after life feels like,  then put on a paracute
goupinaplane, shoot a good amount of heroine
                              immediately
      into your veins and follow that with
      a hit of nitrous oxide then jump.
      or, set yourself on fire.


                                    youre

IN Bloom
Polly
SAPPY
Imodium
PAY to play
Somethings in the WAY
Verse chorus Verse
Sliver
P-ROCK
Lithium

Girl
IN Bloom
Imodium
~~Lithium~~ PAY to play
P-Rock
Lithium

BOY
Sliver
verse chorus verse
SAPPY
Polly
~~Somethings~~ in the WAY

# Give the Gift of music

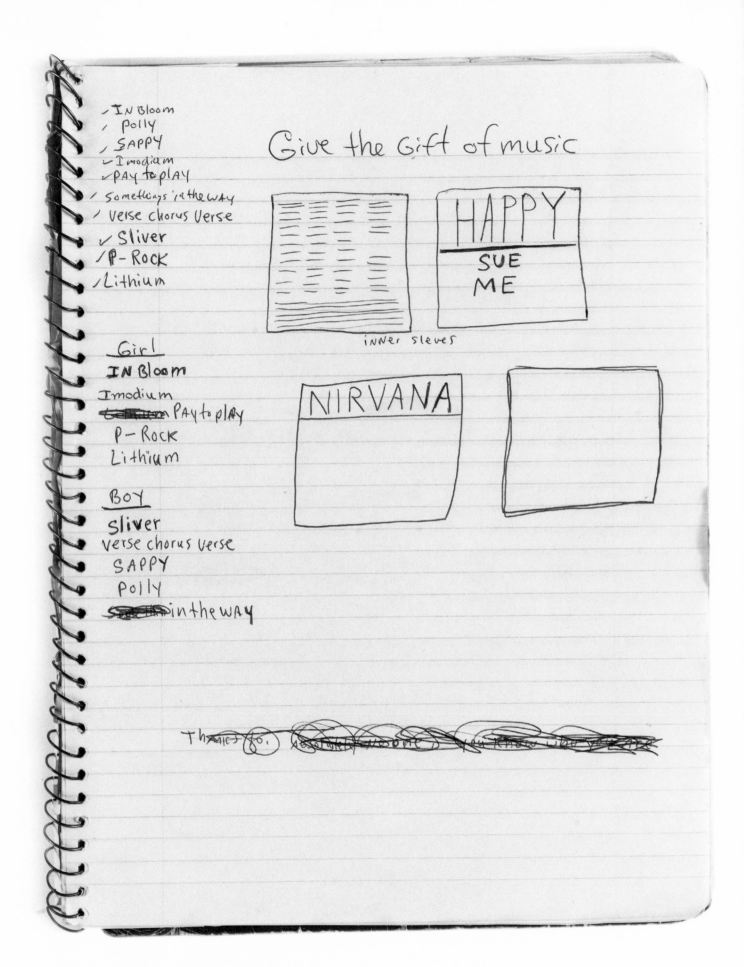

HAPPY
SUE
ME

inner sleves

NIRVANA

Thanks to, ~~asshole awesome you know who you are~~

127

Please send me all Daniel Johnston cassettes

| | | | |
|---|---|---|---|
| H | Blew | | Neg crepe |
| H | School | | IN Bloom |
| S | About A Girl | | Lithium |
| H | IN Bloom | | About A Girl |
| H | Pay to Play | | ~~Imodium~~ Pay to Play |
| S | ~~Polly~~ | | School |
| H | Imodium | | ~~Blew~~ Polly |
| H | Dive | | Dive |
| SH | Lithium | | SAPPY |
| S | SAPPY ~~Bye Bye~~ | | Imodium |
| | To fellow Punk Rockers | | Neg crepe |
| | | | Blew |

for those of you who have been forming ties
with us since the last album, we apologize
for putting ~~these~~ old songs on this LP.
you may consider it a rip off or greatest hits album,
but for those of you who haven't heard our other LP
and the ones who aren't as fortunate as at
liberty to be subject to this self kind of stuff.
~~spare the corpse~~ the limitability of an intelligent toilet.
in other words you have to break in the sheep
with tender loving care. use protection & or vaseline.

NIRVANA SAYS

Thanks to Sonic Youth, mudhoney           Babes in Toyland
SUBPOP, TAD, Fluid, Vaselines, Pixies, melvins, young Marble Giants, STP,
Beat Happening K records, scratch acid, Flipper, BLACK FLAG, BLACK SABBATH,
marine girls, stooges, Butthole Surfers, Beatles, the who, the shaggs, velvet underground,
JANDEK, Daniel Johnston, the KNACK, Swans, Go team, Huddie leadbetter, sonics, screaming trees,
Dead moon, wipers, fang, Gang of four, patsy cline, marlene Dietrich, killdozer,
Saccharin trust, Alice cooper, Devo, B-52's, Blue cheer, shocking Blue, Lee Hazlewood, Half JAPANESE,
Neil Young, Dinosaur Jr, Isaac Hayes, leonard cohen, Ventures, monkees, CCR, Aerosmith, led zep,
Big Black, Gyuto monks, sex pistols, MDC, Queen, Die krenzen, Hüsker Dü, BAD BRAINS, Jimi Hendrix,
Ramones, saints, Blondie, Sgt Barry Sadler, Billie Holiday, Shonen knife, Red Cross, Johnny Cash,

inside sleeve cardboard stencil of visible man
to encourage promotion & vandalism

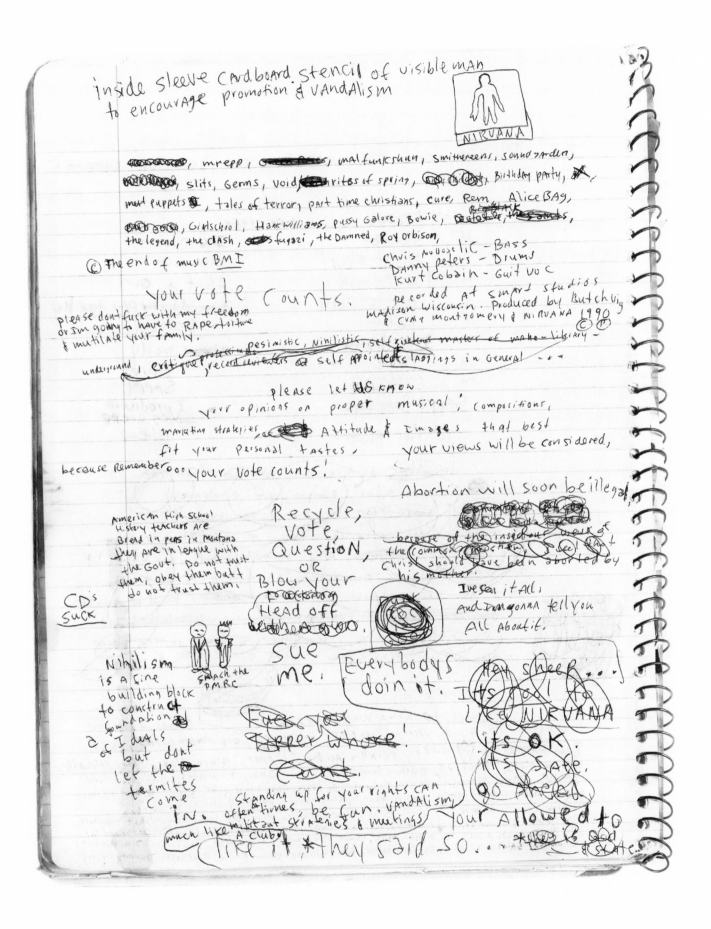

NIRVANA

~~xxxxxx~~, mrepp, ~~xxxxxx~~, malfunkshun, smithereens, soundgarden,
~~xxxxxx~~, slits, germs, void, ~~xxxx~~ rites of spring, ~~xxxxxx~~ Birthday party, ~~x~~,
meat puppets ~~x~~, tales of terror, part time christians, cure, Rem, Alice BAg,
~~xxxxx~~, Girlschool, Hank williams, pussy galore, Bowie, ~~xxxxx~~ ~~xxxxx~~,
the legend, the clash, ~~xxxx~~ fugazi, the Damned, Roy orbison,

© The end of music BMI

Chris novoselic - Bass
Danny peters - Drums
Kurt Cobain - Guit voc

your vote counts.

recorded at smart studios
madison wisconsin. Produced by Butch vig
& craig montgomery & NIRVANA 1990 © ℗

please don't fuck with my freedom
or I'm going to have to RApe, torture
& mutilate your family.

understand & critique ~~professing~~ pesimistic, Ninilistic, self righteous masters of maho-library -
record reviewers @ self appointed class ~~lasdings~~ in general · · ·

please let us know
your opinions on proper musical, compositions,
marketing strategies, ~~xxx~~ Attitude & Images that best
fit your personal tastes, your views will be considered,
because remember ··· your vote counts!

Abortion will soon be illegal,

American High school
History teachers Are
Bred in peas in Montana
they are in league with
the Gout. Do not trust
them, obey them butt
do not trust them.

Recycle,
Vote,
Question,
OR
Blow your
~~xxxxx~~
Head off
~~xxxxx~~.
sue
me.

because of the inside out work of
the common ~~xxx~~ ~~xx~~ see, Butt
chris should have been aborted by
his mother.

I've seen it All,
And I'm gonna tell you
All about it.

CD's
SUCK

Nihilism
is a fine
building block
to construct
foundation
of Ideals
but dont
let the
termites
come
in.

SMASH the
PMRC

~~Fuck you~~
~~xxxxx~~ whore!
~~xxxxx~~.

Everybodys
doin it.

Hey sheep...
Its ok I
Like NIRVANA
its O.K.
its safe.
go ahead

standing up for your rights can
offentimes be fun, vandalism,
much like militant strategies & meetings
A club?

your allowed to
like it * they said so... ~~xxx~~ & skate...

I started it first
I started it first
I I was me
me
I'm the one
I was the Originator
I'll take the blame
me
it was me
I was the instigator
the grandfather
the first and foremost
I was doin it long
Before Anyone
It was me
I'll take all the blame
I'll take full responsibility/
my fault
I started it all
I started it first
me
I'm the one
Blame me
point the finger at me
Heres my receipt
where do I sign?
give me whats owed to me
give me whats rightfully mine
give me what I deserve

# I Deas for Video

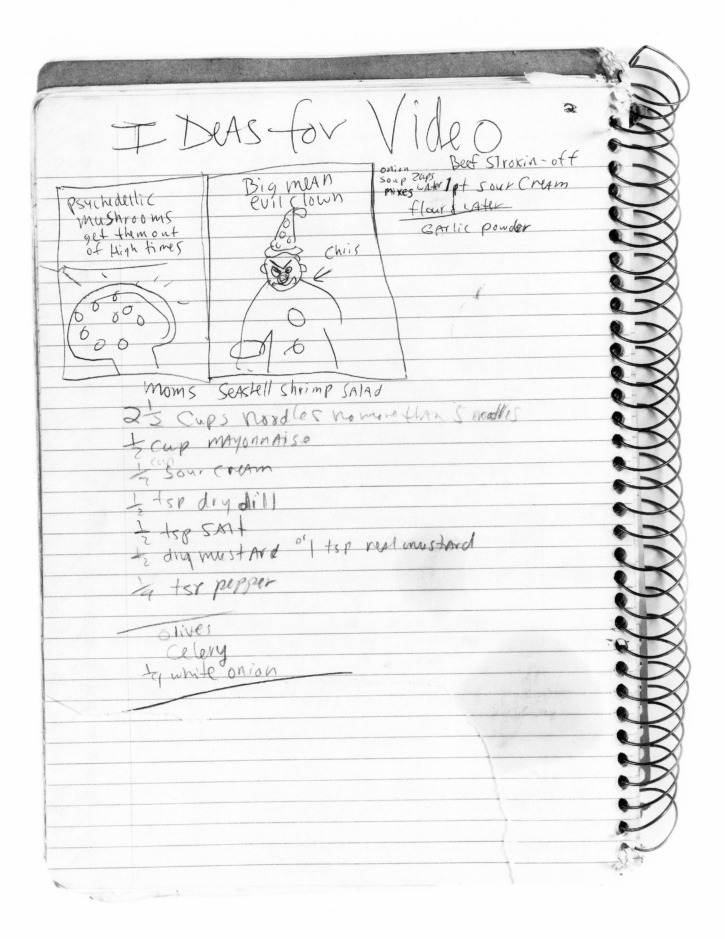

Psychedellic mushrooms get them out of High times

Big mean evil clown

Chiis

onion soup mixes 2 cups water 1 pt sour cream

Beef STrokin-off

flour & LATER

Garlic powder

moms Seastell shrimp salad

$2\frac{1}{3}$ cups noodles no more than 5 needles

$\frac{1}{2}$ cup mayonnaise

$\frac{1}{2}$ cup sour cream

$\frac{1}{2}$ tsp dry dill

$\frac{1}{2}$ tsp salt

$\frac{1}{2}$ dry mustard or 1 tsp real mustard

$\frac{1}{4}$ tsr pepper

olives
celery
$\frac{1}{4}$ white onion

@

K
1 ms  2 Hence 3 Bitch 4 Reynolds  Patti flaeless  stinky  montesano  Fixing same  5   6 | 9  7 Junior High
8  uncle chuck & Joan  summer  monte  grandpa cobain  grandma  9 uncle Jim  10 mom  11  gresky entish  12

It is time now for all the "fortunate"
ones, the cheerleaders and the football
jocks to strip down naked in front of
the entire school at an assembly and
plead with every ounce of their souls
for mercy and forgiveness, to
admit that they are wrong. They
are representatives of Gluttony and selfish
animalistic values and to say that they
are sorry for condoning these things
will not be enough, they must mean
it, they must have guns pointed to their
heads, they must be petrified to ever
think of being the stuck up, self righteous,
segregating, guilt spreading, ass kissing, white,
right wing republicans of the future.


# Kill the Rockefellers

In Bloom
Lithium                    gotta find A WAY, A better WAY
Polly                        to find A way
✝ P Rock
Imodium                  What I need
                              Someday
                              memoria
Pay to Play              Spank Thru
Sliver                   ✝ Lounge Act
Been A son              Second time
Sappy                    I don't have the Right
✦ Verse Chorus Verse    Dumb
✦ Something in the way   Libido
              P-Rock    momma

just because your paranoid
doesn't mean they're not after you

US out of America CANADA
US out of

God is Gay and so Am I

God is love  love is blind and so Am I

I have no opinions
because I agree with everyone

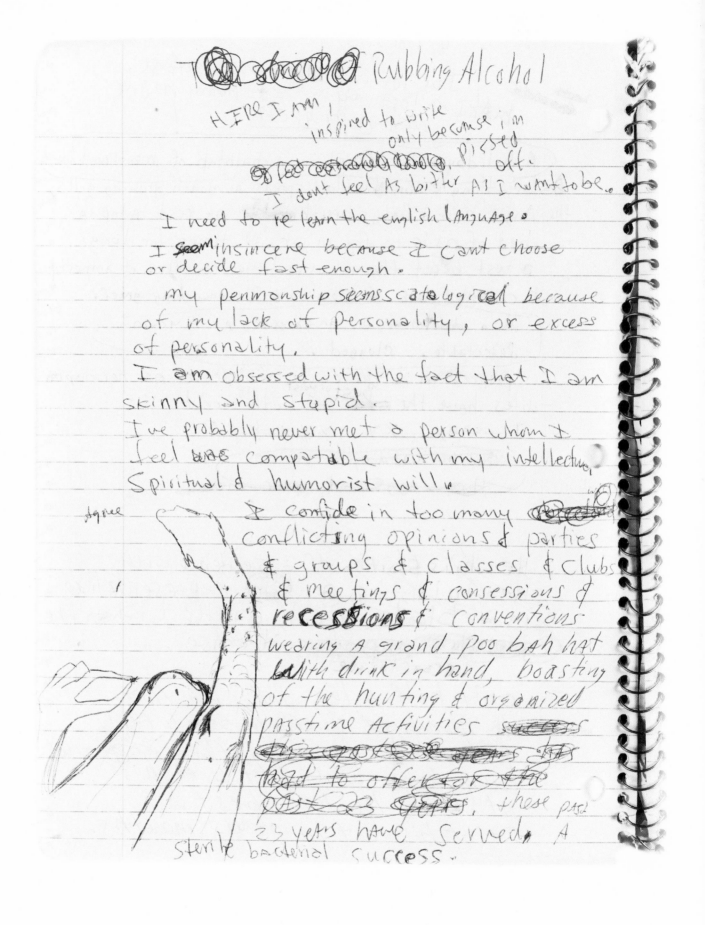

~~○○○○○○○~~ Rubbing Alcohol

HERE I AM,
    inspired to write
        only because i'm
            ~~○○○○○○○○○○~~ pissed off.
        I dont feel As bitter As I want to be.

I need to re learn the english LAnguage.

I ~~seem~~ insincere because I cant choose
or decide fast enough.

    my penmanship ~~seems scatological~~ because
of my lack of personality, or excess
of personality.

I am obsessed with the fact that I am
skinny and stupid.

I've probably never met a person whom I
feel ~~was~~ compatible with my intellectual,
Spiritual & humorist will.

Agree                    I confide in too many ~~○○○○~~
                conflicting opinions & parties
                & groups & classes & clubs
                & meetings & consessions &
                **recessions** & conventions
                wearing A grand poo bah hat
                ~~wi~~th drink in hand, boasting
                of the hunting & organized
                passtime Activities ~~success~~
                ~~these pastyears this~~
                ~~had to offer for the~~
                ~~past 23 years~~, these past
                23 years have served, A
sterile bacterial success.

I've been to A lot of BAd poetry readings

Congratulations to Obsession, ~~sands like perfume isn't~~ extracted from disemboweled whale blubber anymore. Chemicals are the thing of today, today ill take as many chemicals as I can get my greasy paws on, because this scent reminds me of you. just like they said it would in the commercial. yesterdays scent is still here today, Im beached. flat out stranded and obsessed. Ive got to leave because your still here in my Air, fucking with my sense of smell, invading my air waves. your All over the sheets & in the bathroom, my couch REAICS of YOU! ~~~~ you've left your underwear & COAT & records & books & scent here, IN MY ~~~~ place of recovery. the place where I've crawl off to die like A cat under A house After he's been hit, ~~~~ lying around writing

DAVE
(213) 654.              ) I dont invent subjects
                           of interest for conversation,
I dont have Anything to SAY or ASK, I
Just play Along. I'm A reactionary
in A WAY. I just react to what others
SAY. I dont think & when I do I forget.
    give me A leonard cohen Afterworld.

135

# Opinion

Congratulations you have won — it's a
years subscription of bad puns — and a
makce shift story of concern — And to
set it up before it burns — my
opinion

Now there seems to be a problem here
the scale of emotions seem too clear —
Now they — Rise & fall like wall street stock
And they — Have an affect on our peace talks
my opinion

# MANDATORY BREEDING LAWS
## Sue ME
MANDATORY Abortion  VACCINATIONS Denied

~~Taking time to smear dignified street smart~~
~~honest into the carefully cultivated image they~~
~~over represented~~, Now faced with corporate trust,
merging this happy day, This day giving amnesty
to sacrilege. Only do I think when inspiration
is so welcome ~~turne~~ from the allowance you
give with the birth of ~~Grammar~~. Barely beyond
Pissy complaints of ~~description~~ Tongue. Inspired,
I sway back and forth between taking advantage
of my position and giving up. Self appointed
judges of review giving those with similar profit and
potential the confidence to quit.
   So your parents suck. ~~Suicide?~~
parents have always sucked. So your parents
are really pretty cool? ~~Suicide~~ So what! Other kids
parents suck so fight for them. Revolution
is no longer an embarrasement, ~~to be cool~~
thanks to inspiration. The politbureau
questions sarcasm: maintain we must our ~~duty~~
~~All ready to~~ righteously ~~opinions~~ alternative opinions
carved into our
freshman year, and slowly solidifying into the
~~Jimmy Buffet / Jones~~ Taylor kingdom by graduations end.
**JACKSON BROWN**
   At times its an excuse to delay the world
we eventually take in the ass.
   Throw eggs at your enemy. Symbolic chicken foetus
AT Pro lifers.

I am a male, age 23 and I'm Lactating. My breasts have never been so sore not even after receiving ~~Titty~~ twisters from bully-school mates. They had hair down there long before I stopped playing with dolls. I haven't masturbated in months because I've lost my imagination. I close my eyes and I see my father, little girls, german shephards & TV news commentators; but no voluptuous, pouty lipped, naked-~~female~~ sex ~~Kittens~~ wincing in ecstasy from the ~~illusory~~ illusory positions I've conjured up in my mind. No, when I close my eyes I see lizards & flipper babies, the ones who were born deformed because their mothers took bad birth control pills, ~~in the sixties~~

I'm seriously afraid to touch myself.

Homage or Ripoff? I dont care, uh, I dont know.
Seems like finally the appreciation of things are
in order. there are a lot of things & bands to
be thankful for, yes, and everything sucks.
Too many compilations of present day bands paying
homage to old influential bands, Either
there are no good ones left to look forward to
or finally the undergrounds p-rock admittance
to appreciation instead of Everything Sucks!
Clones of old, and the younger generation
never hardly heard old Aerosmith records or Rod Stewart
& Small faces so they have no real sense of
pladgurism in the "now" bands paying homage
(supposedly) or keeping the faith.

Six strings, 24 notes
that repeat the same scale after 10, usually based
on 4'4 time signature, Rock and Roll: 30 years
= Exhausted! Ah the good old days!
The Now generation: recessive unaware recession,
Technology finally caught up with us.
Hiphop/RAP? = for the time being, yes good
at least original; exhausted in 3 years.
women? yes. oppressed from chance
since beginning. probably some ideas left in
an unsaturated vagina.
Record store chains and Radio play it
safe, target audience, what sells,
were completely at their mercy
it used to be the other way around.
Programmers & DJs: get into
Real estate!

139

I am in absolute and total support of: homosexuality, drug use, in experimentation (although I am living proof of harmful results from over indulgence) Anti oppression, ie "(religion, racism, sexism, censorship and patriotism) creativity through music, art, journalism, writing Love, friendship, family, animals and full scale revolution violently resist organized, terrorist-fueled revolution.

You cannot de-program the Glutton. You can only make them scared shitless to. It would be nice to see the gluttons become so commonly violently attacked hunted down that they eventually they will either submit to the opposite of their ways or be scared shitless to ever leave their homes.

John lennon has been my Idol all of my life but he's dEAd wrong about revolution.

Sit on your ass and be beaten!

Bullshit!, Arm yourself, find a representative of Gluttony or oppression and blow the motherfuckers head off. design manifestos with ideas, contacts, recruits, go Public, risk jail or Assasination, get employed by the target so its easier to infiltrate the system slowly get the mechanics of the empire

Hi Eugene,
Its eight o clock in the morning, that means its almost time for bed.

I'm on this rediculous sleeping schedule where I retire in the wee hours of morning and successfully avoid any hint of daylight. my skin is ~~death~~ 90th rock pale. I dont know if you have these things in Scottland but I'm considering joining a tanning bed salon, they are coffin/beds with haloid or flourescent light bulbs built into the sides and lid. ~~and~~ You lye down inside ~~to~~ fry away turning a crisp golden brown. we call them nuclear tans.

Lately my nipples have been really sore, can males lactate? How have you been?

As you probably know, we recorded mollyslips & son of a gun for a peel session and we were wondering if we could use the recordings for a promotional EP hopefully to be released in a few months. We dont expect to make a profit off of it because were keeping the price down, It's mainly a feature for our supposedly hip-alternative debut single 'IN Bloom', the EP will have (if consented) ~~and~~ (PLUS) IN Bloom, Sliver, D-7 by the wipers, Turn around by Devo, ~~and~~ mollys lips and maybe son of a gun. If we do make any money off of this then we'll surely devide it amongst the bands or we could talk about up front advance for the use of the songs or whatever, it's legit!

were not on Sub Pop any more, our new label is DGC (Geffen)
we are label mates with <u>Nelson</u>!

I know this is starting to sound too business like
but I want you to have something for
giving us this ~~scribbled out~~
    great honor ~~scribbled out~~
to play your songs, they mean a lot
    to me. without trying to be too embarvasingly
Sappy ~~scribbled out~~ I have to say the songs you
and frances have written are some of
the most beautiful songs ever and I just
feel like everyone should hear them.
Heres what the Cover might look like ⟶

I had a really fine time
at the show we played together
the video turned out good. you
want a copy? oh yeah, European
Video format, forget it.    geez I
Tape
dont know what else to say.
    please write me (if you want)
        and let me know how your
new band is coming along and
anything else thats on your mind.

            Love, your pal
            kurdt

NIRVANA sings
the Vaselines
wipers
Devo
&
NIRVANA

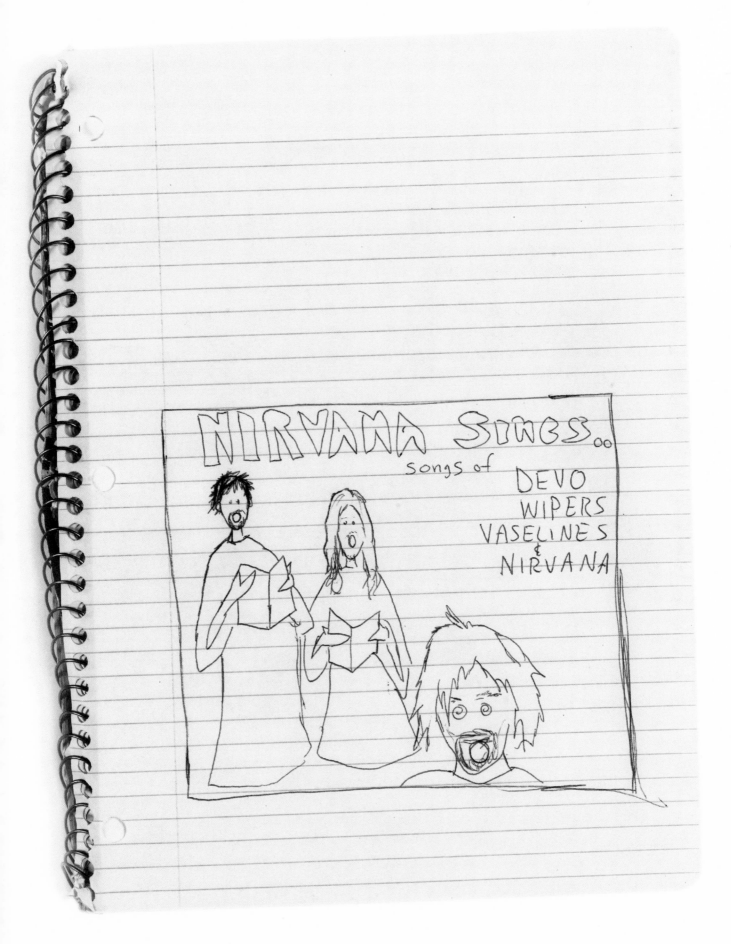

Bill price — guns & roses     Chris thomas   engineer     sex pistols

Gill Norton  pixies

Allan moulder — my bloody valentine   mixed   Jesus & Mary Chain

? & BARbiAro —  guns roses soundgarden

George Derkoulios —  BLACK crowes     available last week of June

John Hanlon —  Ragged glory  freedom

Dave Jerden —  James Addiction   Talking Heads   Alice n Chains

Cd StAsium —   living Colour

Ron St Jermin — Anthrax  Death Angel   the youth


Scott Litt

And HAiry, sweaty, macho-sexist and racist Dickheads who
will soon drown in a pool of razor blades and sperm from
the uprising of your children, the armed and de-programmed
crusade, littering the floors of WALL Street with revolutionary debris,
Assassinating both the lesser and greater of two evils, ~~getting~~ — Botanical
~~absolute~~ bringing an everlasting sterile and bacterial, herbaceous & corporate
cleansing for our ancestors to gaze in wondernment and awe.
The representatives of the American male rApes
in more WAYS than one.
~~or well whatever, nevermind~~

posing as the enemy to infiltrate the mechanics of the empire
and slowly start it's rot from the inside
it's an inside job — it starts with the custodians And
the cheerleaders, oh well, whatever, nevermind.

*(left margin):* will be strung up by their BALLS with pages of the Scum manifesto stapled to their Bodys

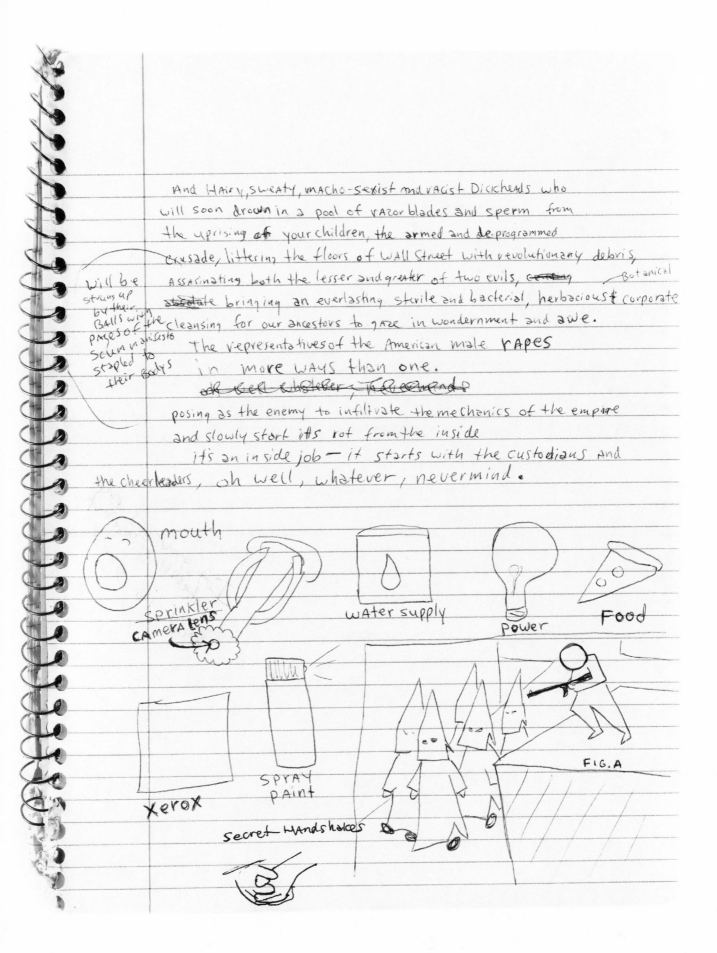

mouth

sprinkler
CAMERA lens

water supply

Power

Food

Xerox

SPRAY PAint

secret HANDshakes

FIG. A

Cursed Aint the word

# smells like Teen Spirit

It will
be fun

Come out and play - make up the rules
have lots of fun  we know we'll lose

PPY
PLANTS
are
growing

Our little group has always been and
always will until the end

pep
Assemblys
Become
RALLYS

The other biggest ones  dont deserve
to know  oh no  I told a secret word
        A  Dirty word
                              Bend

revolutionary
debris
litters the
floor of
WallStreet,
your
children
have
taken
over,
you
have
been
warned.

load up on guns & bring your friends
I know I know  lets not  pretend  it's wrong to
Take off your clothes I'll see you in court  offend

Secret
Humashales

Is what you should  Abort
                              Abort

Club

We merge ahead this special day
this day giving Amnesty to sacrilege

the
representatives
of gluttony
and All the other
netto things that
are related
will be given
24 hours to
VACCUM
and shave
their ways
or leave,
or they
will be
weeded out

flyers
fly

Learn All three chords
down your competition is weak

get out of bed itall a deep

store

Hoard

And Assasinated
with A HO
to the back
of the neck

to save
Bullets

A gift of Choice I got from you

oh No I know A Dirty word

~~I'll take as much As you can I never know~~
~~when youll run out~~

                   got from you

blemish
blush
     Now I forget just why I taste - oh yeah
         I guess   It makes me smile
what is
     why dont you cry when I'm ~~~~ AWAY
     oh yeah  we want whats best for you
touch
the truth
truth
      ___ ___ repeat    is something New
I don't
remember

     The finest day Ive ever had

     WAS when Tomorrow Never came
     I'm ~~~~ bad at what I do best
           Im blessed to know  ~~Fame~~
   And for this gift I feel blessed  that Most Are
                           Tame

     my credit ran away from me

with the light out It's less dangerous
Here we are now entertain us
I feel stupid And contagious
Here we Are now  Segregate us

A mulato    An Albino
A mosquito    my Libido
        YAY


come hang yourself with Umbilicle Noose



uH oh  oh No  A Dirty word

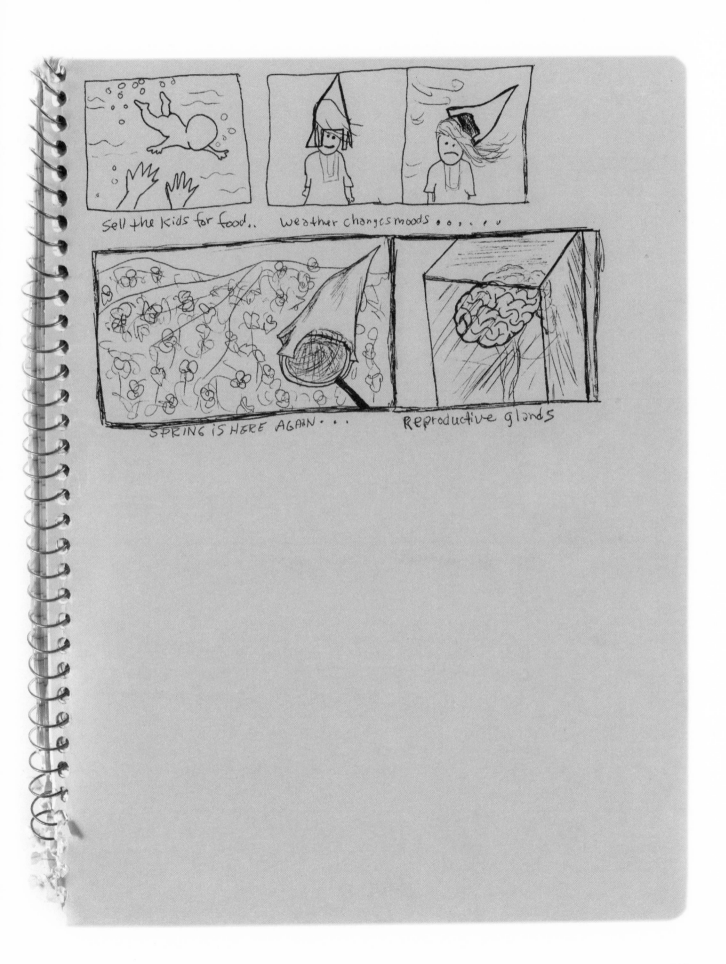

# Lithium

① * Im so happy because today I found my friends
Theyre in my Head.

* Im so ugly but thats ok cause so Are you
~~And~~ ~~we~~ We broke our mirrors

Sunday morming is ~~the da~~ everyday for All I care
And Im ~~not sad scared~~ not scared
Light my candles ~~in a daze~~ cause I found God
Hey Hey Hey

Im so lonely but thats ok I shaved your head
And Im not sad

And Just maybe
Im to blame for All Ive heard but Im not sure
                    excited
Im so ~~hateful~~ I cant wait to meet you
there - but I dont care

Im so horny thats ok my will is good
And ~~Ive got food~~ to tie ~~me over~~ and
~~Keep my mind~~ on ~~meeting you~~
~~And eat my friends~~ ~~Again and~~ Again

I ~~Like~~ you  } Im not gonna crack
I miss you  }
I love you
I Killed you

night flight
11811 west olympic Blvd
Los Angeles
CA 90064

# smells like teen spirit

(feel)

Come out and play, make up the rules   so stupid
~~I know I hope to buy~~ the truth

Take off your clothes I'll see you in court
~~[scribbled out]~~
~~Hello Hello~~ ~~hello~~
~~We know~~ we'll lose ~~but~~ we wont be bored   YAY group
Come out and play, make up the rules
~~Its not enough with golden tools~~
Dyslexic idiot savant with bad hearing
load up on Guns & bring your friends
The secret hand shakes pretend
~~we're so stupid~~ so lazy, ~~blame our parents~~
~~[scribbled] fazes me~~
Neurotically   ~~we're so lazy & so stupid~~        So famous
LA-thargic   ~~blame our parents~~   entertaining your pamphlet   has been read
~~the stupids~~         every night before bed
Tribe   variety   Undeserving

our little group has always been, and always will
until the end                    swore
We cut our hands & made a pact ~~then~~ were never going back

Tribe
Territory
~~Leaving~~ Pissings
Spraying
Your mark

A mulato    an Albino
A mousquito    my Libido

YAY    A deposit
for A bottle
stink inside it
No Role model

A Denial

It's always
been and always will until the end

The same percent

say anything
just to have an
opinion

Who will be the King & Queen
of the Outcasted ~~[scribbled]~~ teens
I hate to use percentages It's nice to know there is
A choice

151

# IN BLOOM

Sell the kids for food - weather
changes moods

Spring is here Again - Re-Productive
glands

Hes the one who likes all the
pretty Songs - and he likes to sing
along - and he likes to shoot his
Gun    But he knows not
what it means    know not
what it means and I SAY AAHH

We can have some more
Nature is A whore
Bruises on the fruit
Tender Age in Bloom

I SAW Jesus's face in wood panelling          Tastes like chicken

# Verse chorus Verse

Lucky BLACK sheep BLACKMAILed
I'll see you in court
I was so High that I scratched
until I Bled
At the end of RAinbows and
~~the end~~ of your Rope
I was drawn into the
mAgnet TAR pit ~~~~ P~~ool~~

Grass is greener over here
LeAds to ~~~~ burning bridges cleAr
Reinventing what we knew
I cant wait until im sued    —

your the reason i feel pain
it feels so good to feel again

SAline on the ocean in A Tank of fumes
wheres my stamp collection? I'm becoming bored
Have another baby its not filled up yet
IveLostAllmy contacts and my LACK of Iron
I SAW Jesus image in wood parelling

collect prepaid postage PAID
send bill
A three Hour tour
Boning jests
Buy my Bottled sweat
He goes without saying
SPAyed & neutered
LACK of Iron

# Verse Chorus Verse

Neither side is sacred - No one wants to
win - feeling so sedated think I'll just
give in - Taking medication till my
stomachs full - I'm A moody **BABY**


grass is greener - over here -
youre 1

Reinventing what we knew
I cant wait until im sued

Drain you
feels like                          Power

Come As you are

Come as you are - as you were -
As I want you to be -
as a friend - as a friend - as an
old enemy - Take your time -
hurry up - the choice is yours -
dont be late - take a rest -
as a friend - as an old -
memoria    memory  ah

Come dowsed in mud - Soaked in Bleach
As I want you to be -
As a Trend as a friend as an old
enemy memoriah

You said that i remind you of yourself tomorrow

And I swear that I don't have a Gun

155

# Lounge Act

You. – keepin everything in line
mastering the Art to remind
begging me to lighten up
never seems to be enough
    Lounging in the sea
    and I've got this

I burnt my hands so I can't feel
I'll wet my bed to make you a deal
I'll gouge my eyes
I'll wear High Heels
I'll wrack my brains to prove I can still
    smell Him on you

You – wishin everything Away
Bring it back Another day

Safety is A special suit
cover up A Home

# ON A PLAIN

I'll start this off without any words
I got so High that I scratched till I bled

The finest day that I've ever had
was when I learned to cry on command

Chorus ( I love myself Better than you I know its
wrong so what should I do

my mother died every night
Its safe to say dont quote me on that

The Black sheep got black mailed again
Forgot to put on the zip code

It is now time to make it unclear
to write off lines that don't make sense

Somewhere I have heard this before
IN A dream my memory has stored
As defense I'm Neutered & spayed
What the Hell Am I trying to say?

one more special message to go
And then I'm done then I can go home

I'm on a plain I cant complain
I'm on a plane I cant complain

157

# mead

VERSE
CHORUS
VERSE
CHORUS
Solo
Chorus
Chorus

5 CXL 6
PAY 'n SAVE
199

120 sheets/college ruled
11x8½in/27.9x21.6cm

# 3 subject
# notebook

06710   The Mead Corporation, Dayton, Ohio 45463

Hi, I'm 24 years old. I was born a white, lower middle class male off the coast of WAshington state. My parents owned a compact stereo component system molded in simulated wood grain CASing and A ~~5~~ record box set ~~of~~featuring Am rAdios contemporary Hits of the eArly seventies CAlled 'good vibrations' by Ronco. It had such hits as tony orlando & DAwns 'tie A yellow ribbon' and Jim Croche's time in a bottle. After years of *my* begging they finally bought me a tin drumset with paper heads out of the BACK of A SeArs catalog. Within the first week my sister poked Holes in the heAds with A screwdriver.

I cried to "seAsons in the sun".

My mother played A song by chicago on our piano, I don't remember the name of the song but I'll never forget the melody.

my Aunt gave me a *blue* Hawaiian slide guitar and Amp for my 7th birthday, she Also during those first precious yeArs had given me the first 3 beAtles albums for which I am forever grateful knowing that my musical development would have probably ~~Come~~ to A HOLE ~~if~~ ~~~~ *If I had to soak up one more the* of CArpenters and Olivia Newton John.

IN 1976 i found out that the beatles had been broken up since 71 ~~and I had never heard of~~ ~~Jimi Hendrix~~ My parents got a divorce so I moved in with my dad into a trailer park in an even smaller logging community.

My dads friends talked him into joining the Columbia record club and soon records showed up at my trailer Almost once A week Accumulating Quite a ~~large~~ ~~Records by 77~~ collection by 77

what dr? - witt
location? - lakewood community center
9112 ~~Heartsn~~ Lakewood dr Sw

Fig.A

Rooftop

Theres at least one form of social change ~~that~~
~~the early 90's has brought,~~ ~~(scratched out text)~~
~~gain~~ the attainment of finally accepting various styles
~~achieve~~ of music (and/or style of dress) ~~(scratched out text)~~
~~accomplishment~~ Amongst the youth.      This is the first generation
~~unanimity~~ that has brought musical unity between them and their parents.
There ~~today~~ is no generation gap, since the
: AMOK :                    god fearing
                           white bread catho
PO Box 861867      Days of the ~~last~~ 40's
Terminal Annex          Just after the 2nd
                           worldwar,
Los Angeles, CA 90086-1867   Jitterbug
            Boogie    skittle, hand jivin,
            woogie

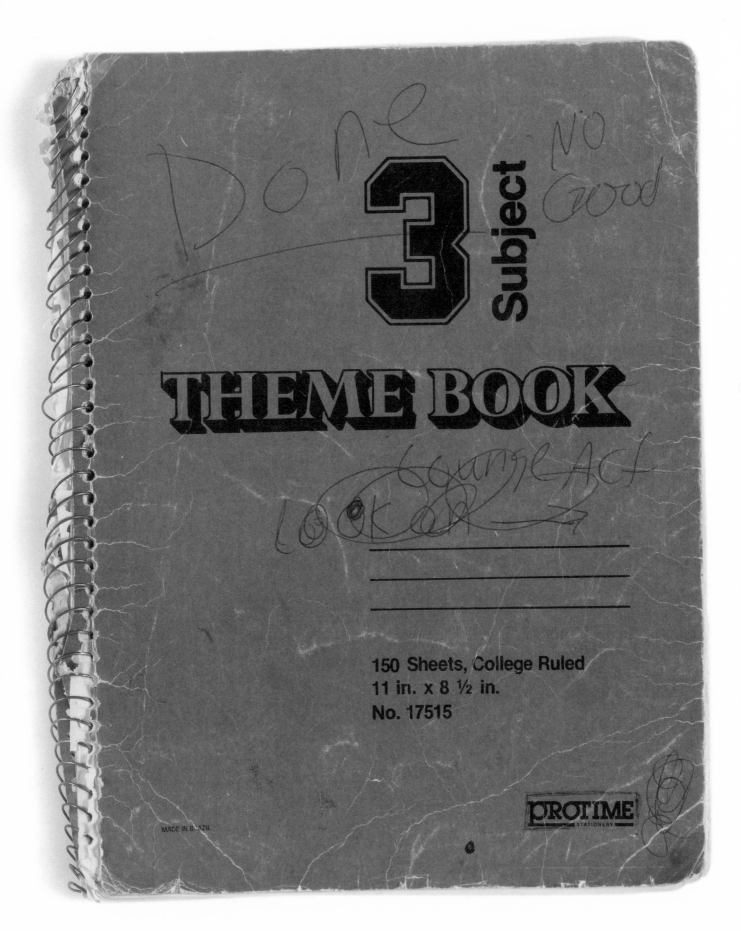

| | |
|---|---|
| Se...s | Smells like Teen Spirit |
| Gross HAPPY (X) | DRAin You |
| HAPPY | Lithium |
| HAPPY | In Bloom |
| SAD (E) | Come As You Are |
| SAD | Polly |
| MAD | Territorial Pissings |
| HAPPY Bleed | (Immodium M Verse chorus Verse) |
| MAD | STAY AWAY |
| SAD | Something in the WAY |
| HAPPY (X) | ON A PLAin |
| HAPPY | Lounge ACT |

NIRVANA

Nevermind

Verse chorus Verse
* SAPPY
Lounge ACT
ON A PLAin
old Age

Thanks to : ~~Alan~~ ~~Jimmy Carter,~~ Jimmy Carter,
Susan Sylvers, ~~~~, chad channing, Danny Peters, the Melvins, Sonic Youth, mudhoney
Bob Goldthwait, the Vaselines, the wipers, the Beatles, the Pixies, Black Flag,
scratch Acid, ~~~~ Leadbelly, Night Flight, the Stooges, ~~~~ 70's ~~~~
~~~~, Olympia, Brothers Quay, Flipper, Devo, Gang of four, aron Berkhart,
~~~~, flipside, Beat Happening, H.R. Puffnstuff, Mark Lanegan,
Tales of Terror, Butthole Surfers, New Wave theatre, REM, young Marble Giants,
Aerosmith, Led Zeppelin, Johnathan Poneman, Bruce Pavitt, TAd
~~Thanks to : Teen Rock~~
~~and everyone were not whether you were good or loved~~
~~you were probably inspiring in one way or another~~

Thanks to: Un-encouraging parents everywhere for giving their children
the will to show them up,  and to the white macho-american
Male for reminding the small percent who are capable of recognizing injustice
to fight you and learn from your sick sadistic instinctual ways
May you rot in the very reason even though you ~~exist to~~ to stay alive whatever
~~~~

Thanks to ~~the representatives of gluttony~~ political figures and
those in the entertainment industry who Are the
representatives of gluttony, for reminding us

    Dont fuck your children
    Dont beat your kids

NEVERMIND

NIRVANA
! ? O ☆
NEVERMIND

165

"Rock is musical freedom. It's saying, doing and playing what you want. Nirvana means freedom from pain and suffering in the external world And that's ~~my~~ close to my definition of punk rock," exclaims guitarist Kurt Kobain. ~~The weight of that grope~~ Nirvana try to fuse punk energy with Hard rock riffs, all within a pop sensibility. "Speaking of sensibility" adds bass guitarist~~s~~ CHRIS NOVOSELIC "I wish we had more sense, you know basic common sense, like rembering to pay your phone bill or rent". With the band inking a deal with D.G.C earlier this year the band is enjoying all the trappings that come with it.

"Trapping, Schmapping fuck it man ~~they~~ throw us A few bones and the lights stay on for a while". rebuffs Drummer Dave Grohl. Cynical of the music industries machinery ~~Th~~ Nirvana still sees the nesscessity ~~to of such an apparatice~~ to drive their musical Crusade.

nevermind the bands second album but 1st on a major label. culminated two years After the release of their first Album BLEACH. "Kurt notes" HAVE you ever had ~~to find a job~~ a day when you were going to find a job then it was already two o'clock so you just blew it off? then the next day a friend comes over and hangs out, so you'll go tomorrow. Then well tomorrow, then tomorrow etc. etc. etc." However during this period the "Procrastination BUG" didn't AFFECT the bands song writing. An E.P. was reliesed BLEW. It had two songs off BLEACH (Love Buzz, BLEW) And two new songs (Been A Son, Stain). In the Fall of '90 the band reliesed the single, SLiver/DIVE. ~~there~~ are also various studio outakes making the rounds on the ~~greasy~~ sleazy Bootleg market.

and two recordings

167

played

Nirvana ~~toured~~ alot also during this period - three major tours, including excursions to England twice and elsewhere in Europe once. They played in Berlin one day after the wall fell. "~~People were crying at the sight of bananas~~" ~~recalls Kobain.~~ "there were westerners offering people coming over baskets of fruit and a guy cried at the sight of bananas". recalls Kobain.

the bands roots go back to '87. It's the classic case of two bored art students dropping out and forming a band. Kobain, a saw blade painter specializing in wildlife and seascapes. Met Novoselic whose passion was glueing sea shells and driftwood on burlap potatoe sacks, at the acclaimed Grays Harbon ~~school of crafts~~ institute of northwest crafts Chris notes "when I saw Kobains work I knew there was something special. I introduced myself to him and asked what his roots were on this ~~glitter dust~~

macaroni mobile piece I
was working on. He suggested
I glue glitter on it. From
then on it was an artistic
partnership that would spawn
the basis of what is the
magical collaboration of Nirvana
today" AFTER A long succesion
of /drummers Nirvana finally
~~XXXXXXXXX~~ ~~XXXXX~~

# smells like
## Teen Spirit

needed
1. mercedes benz and a few old cars
2. Access to a Abandoned mall, main floor and one Jewelry shop.
3. lots of fake Jewelry
4. school Auditorium (Gym)
5. A cast of hundreds. 1 custodian, students.
6. 6 black cheerleader outfits with Anarchy A's (A) on chest

I had a cigarette in my hand, I thought it was a ~~cig~~ pen, I started writing a letter to my congressman, I told him about misery and corruption and bat cave ~~girls~~ — death rock girls who have danced at nude clubs in the city while trying to get off drugs and how they really, really care and if more vegetarian vampires could concentrate on ~~the~~ disclaimer-malpractice, sitting in the dark channelling the ~~c~~ combined energy ~~s~~ of all the lost infant souls in this sphere or realm then we could all sip ~~the~~ licorice-flavored alcoholic beverages down by the lazy rivers of ~~Jordan~~ the rhone or ~~r~~ rhine. I don't have a beef with you, or a terrible, bitter, starvation for or in general. and its really hurting my lungs. this faq is marinated with the fear of the ℃PP and laced with heavy ~~metal~~ metal-power ballads, giving me the clout to use stationary soaked in my favorite perfume and to put a stamp on upside down, only proves how much smell there is here and now, before ancestors and flint or even citrus colored sports bottles. Well, get your priorities straight, ~~you fucker. you mean nasty person~~

His jaw dropped. and off slid his finely sculpted, bohemian goatee.

Breeders - pod    An epic that will never let you forget
your ex girlfriend.

Pixies **surfer rosa** - A die-cast metal fossil from a space craft,
with or without the fucking production.

Leadbellys last sessions (folkways) Vol. 1 - orgones, pyles,
Cells and he probably knew the difference between male
and female hemp.

Vaselines - pink & Green EPS -  Eugene + frances = documented
love.

young Marble Giants - Colossal Youth - lying in an iron lung
filled with luke warm water and epsom salts.

wipers - "is this real?" -  yeah it is.

Shonen knife - Burning Farm EP - when i finally got to see them
live, I was transformed into a hysteric nine year old
girl at a Beatles concert.

Sex pistols - Nevermind the Bollocks - one million times more important than
the clash

Jad fair - great expectations - with my head phones on, Jad
and I ~~share the~~ ~~see~~ share "our little secret"
walking thru shopping malls and Air ports.

YEAH, and then
they wiped their butts with it ~~then~~
set it on fire!

rehabilitation, sympathy: Groups.
usually small, non profit or state funded
organizations directed to ~~helping~~ rape
victims cope with the crime ~~on them.~~
brought upon them, also known as
rape crisis centers or planned parenthood
who by the way have now ~~been~~ just recently
been ~~informed~~ that it ~~now is unlawful~~
soon will be unlawful for doctors ~~at~~
working at these centers (usually on a
voluntary basis) to offer young pregnant
women every option available, meaning:
~~abortion~~ They are not allowed to suggest
the option of abortion,
        ▇▇  I wonder if it was ~~an~~ intentional
~~a~~ decision ~~to leave out such~~ ~~for your~~ part
to ~~leave out such~~ ● vital key word as
such as ~~the~~ sympathy or rehabilitation, instead,
leaving the word 'group' all by its lonesome
to deceivingly make this rediculous little
quote to read as if I were attacking
other groups (meaning Rock Bands)
for inefficiently ~~for~~ addressing rape and in turn
so righteously claiming that the song polly
was ~~intended to~~ written as a rebuttle
towards these groups or (your so-called
(Rock bands) and to claim that ~~this~~
~~(song in any way has effectively~~
our BAND (NIRVANA) have conciously decided that
it is ~~a~~ on devout crusade ~~for us, to~~ as a band,
to ~~teach~~ teach men not to rape. ~~the is totally~~
we find it very frustrating ~~to~~ engage in a 2
Hour in depth interview and to waste these

this
is happening
in the U.S.
so why
should you
care?
it could
probably
happen
there
as
well.

not
print

for
inefficiently

two hours giving what we felt was a pretty insightful interview ~~and~~ then it turns out, only a few embarrasingly misquoted words were used, ~~making it~~ not to mention one quote literally stolen from another article a few months ~~later~~ ago from NME ( guns n roses attack) and in the end making it seem As if were a band who have nothing better to say than garbled-second rate political rantings, we are not politically correct, but yes we do ~~feel~~ have opinions on these ~~matters~~ but we don't deserve the illusive display of ~~the next Guns and roses your more responsible for the exaggerated~~ Commercial Hype

P.S. Being solely A political band, it's quite obvious ~~that~~ were not qualified or prolific enough to even try. thats why 90% of our interviews consist of half witted talk about music or our pets and when squeezed out of us about 10% of sincere, politically personal viewpoints revealed, and why is this? learning the hard way, ~~to~~ not ~~be~~ able to trust the majority of the incestually-competetive english journalist. talk about politics shall we? how many ~~sadistic~~ times have journalists of both papers one another

stabbed in the back, lied or provided favors
in order to beat one another for a cover story
~~of the~~ with the same band? er, just a guess.
sensationalist tabloids are quite harmless and
its understandable why they are needed when
the majority of present rock bands, have
nothing to say musically but ^musical inspiration seems
to have been deformed by the vicious and
self serving pleasure ~~of~~ the journalist which
naturally incites bands to become paranoid
Defensive, jaded, abusive and uncooperative.
the english journalist is a ~~masochistic~~
second rate self apointed judge who couldnt
make it to becoming a ~~therapist~~ mental therapist,
theyre enemic, clammy, physically deformed,
gnome-like, internally upset with a dysfunctional
ability to stabilize a relationship (except
with each other) and sincerely masochistic
who would bathe in the glamour of
nude photos of ~~them selves~~ with handcuffs
behind the back, on their knees wearing
a diaper with a ~~scrunchie~~ rubber
cock stuffed in their mouth~~s~~ and these
photos pasted on every cover magazine
in europe.       the rivals and the poachers
shall one day ban together ~~and~~ print
one tabloid ~~a~~ monthly.

we
gleefully
decline
the
opportunity
to
Be
raped
by
the limey
Journalist.
By saying to
future interviews?
No thanks
No thank
You

and the weak crumbs will report to
the custodial Arts. ~~schools~~

love kur-d-t Koebane

**Hi)**

Yeah, all Isms feed off one another,
but at the top of the food chain is still
the white, corporate, macho, strong
ox~~of~~ male. Not redeemable as far as im
concerned. I mean, classism is determined
by sexism because the male decides whether
~~it~~ it still exists ~~still.~~ its up to men. ~~racism~~
~~sexism etc.~~ Im just saying that people cant deny any ism
or think that some are more or less subordinate.
~~But still think that in order to~~
except for sexism. He's in charge
He decides. I still think that in order
to expand on all other isms, sexism has to
be blown wide open, ~~its like when you~~
Its almost impossible to de program
the incestually-established, male oppressor,
~~but the~~ especially the ones whove been
weaned on it thru their familys generations,
like die hard N.R.A. freaks and inherited,
~~of~~ corporate, power mongrels, the ones whove
were born into no choice but to keep the
torch and only let sparks fall for the rest
of us to gather at their feet. But
there are thousands of Green minds, young
gullable 15 year old Boys out there just
starting to fall into the grain of what
theyve been told of what a man is
supposed to be, and there are plenty of
tools to use, ~~the most~~ the most
effective tool is entertainment. The
entertainment industry is just now

starting to accept us. (mainly because of trendy falseness of environmentally, socially concience hype) ie: the new 90's attitude, which is at a total standstill because of the patriotic, aftermath of the war and all its Nuremberg rally-parades) but they're using mediA!! Media. Major labels, ( (the evil corporate Oppressors, ( god I nud a new word!) the ones who are in KAhoots with the government, the ones the underground movment went into retaliation against in the early 80's) The corporations are finally allowing subversive supposedly subversive, alternative thinking bands to have a loan of money to expose their crusade, ~~with their~~ obviously they arent ~~doing too~~ forking out loans for this reason, but more because it looks to be a money making, comodity, but we can use them! we can pose as the enemy to to infiltrate the mechanics of the system to start its rot from the inside. sabotage the empire by pretending to play their game, compromise just enough to call their bluff. And the hairy, sweaty, MACHO, sexist dickheads will soon drown in a pool of razor blades and semen, stemmed from the uprising of their children, the armed and deprogrammed crusade, littering the floors of WAllstreet with revolutionary debris. Assasinating both the lesser and greater of two evils. bringing an everlasting, sterile and bactereal herbacious and botanical and corporate cleansing for our

ancestors to gaze in wonderment and Awe, AWE!
geezus christ. (repeat): poring as the enemy
to infiltrate the mechanics of the empire and
slowly start its rot from the inside, its an
inside job - it starts with the custodians
and the cheerleaders. And ends with the entertainers.
The youth are waiting, impatiently.
Homophobe VACCECTOMY.
    Its like what Allen said about how in school
there was this class that you went to and they
were teaching the girls how to prepare themselves
for rape and when you looked outside and saw
the rapers outside playing football and
you said "they are the ones who should be in
here being taught not to rape".
    How true. Suck em in with quality
entertainment and hit em with reality.
The revolution will be televised.
        Theres this new 24 hour channel on cable called
the 90s, which is available only in a few states so far
and it's magazine version can be seen on Pbs
(public broadcasting system) once a week
    it's pretty damn informative and it exposes
injustices in a kind of conservative-
/liberal format, but its new so it has to be that
way. Ive seen it a few times and really liked
it. Also Night flight is back. you know,
the show that used to play newwave theatre?
        We plan to use these shows and others
if given the chance. Yeah I know, I'm a
Confused, uneducated, walking cliche, but I dont need
to be inspired any longer, just supported.

Oh yeah, Gluttony, I almost forgot Gluttony.
The band now has an image: the anti-
gluttony, materialism & consumerism image
which we plan to incorperate into all of our
videos. The first one 'Smells like teenspirit'.
will have us walking through a mall throwing
thousands of dollars into the air as mall-goers
scramble like vulchers to collect as much
as they can get their hands on, then we walk
into a jewelry store & smash it up in anti-
materialist ~~~~~~ fueled, punk rock violence.
~~~~~~ then we go to A Pep
Assembly at a High school And the cheerLeaders
have (A)narchy A's on their sweaters and the
custodian-militant-revolutionarys hand out guns with
flowers in the barrels to all the cheering
students who file down to the center court
and throw their money & jewelry & Andrew dice
Clay Tapes into A big pile then we
set it on fire and run out of the
building screaming. Oh, didn't twisted sister
already do this?
        Things that have been taken from
me within the past 2 months:    1 wallet, drivers
license etc., $2,100ºº three guitars (including
the moserite) all my neato 70's effect boxes,
apartment and phone.    but ~~~~~ I got
a really neato left handed Fender Jaguar which
is, in my opinon, almost as cool as a mustang.
    So I consider it a fair trade for the moserite

180

while staying in L.A.
We almost got killed by gang members.
well, sort of.
Dave Franz and I were in the parking lot
of a famous, female-mudwrestler-night club
scoring lewds, when all of a sudden two
gass guzzling cars pulled up next to us and
five cho-los with knives and guns walked
over to the car closest to ours and started yelling
& cursing in gang lingo at eachother. But then
by the motto of "To protect and serve" the
cops show up, which insighted the gang
bangers to flee away in their cars, resulting
in a hot persuit - Car Chase. There were
even hellicopters with search lights.
Needless to say we scored our lewds and
split.       We played a really fun show with
fitz of Depression at a really small coffee house
called the jabberjaw.       we were indescribably
fucked up on booze and drugs, out of tune
and rather uh, sloppy. It took me
about fifteen minutes to change my guitar
string while people @ heckled and called
me drunk Robyn Zander. (cheap trick lead singer?)
After the show I ran outside and vomited.
then I came back in to find Iggy pop there
so I gave him A sloppy-puke breath kiss'
and hug.  He's A really friendly and cool
and nice and interesting person. It was probably
the most flattering moment of my life.

As you may have guessed by now I've been taking a lot of drugs lately.

It might be time for the Betty ford clinic or the Richard Nixon library to save me from abusing my enemic, rodent-like body any longer. I cant wait to be back at home (wherever that is) in bed, neurotic and malnourished and complaining how the "weather sucks" and its the whole reason for my misery. I miss you, Bikini Kill.

I totally love you.

Kurdt

There is a small percent of the population
who were **BORN** with the ability to
detect injustice. they have Tendencies
to question injustice and to look for
answers (by their oppressors standards in ways. that would
be considered abnormal. They have Tendencies
and talents in the sense that they know from
an early age that they have the gift to
challenge what is expected of their future.

These kids are usually hyperactive, uncontrollable
brats who never know when to quit because their
so wrapped up in whatever their trying to prove,
that they eventually offend someone, not meaning
to of course. This is good.

They usually go through childhood thinking
their special. its partly instinctual or maybe
they've been told by their parents or teachers,
maybe they're put in a gifted childrens —
over achiever class in grade school. for whatev
reason they end up molding into a person
aware of their abilities and not understanding
them and having bloated egos caused by
societys insistance that those with an
overly-functional insight should be praised
and considered to be on a higher level of standards
easy access towards success. Eventually
they become totally confused and bitter
adolescents who tend to see nothing but injustice
because by that time they (usually) have
had the chance to be exposed to others
like them who learn from their gifted, bohemian
ancestors.

that their special.

Ancestors

conciousness The larger percent who have and always will dominate the smaller percent *simply because they outnumber* were not **BORN** with even the slightest ability to comprehend injustice. there are the stump dump *AverageJoe* Garbage men *or Lawyers* of life.

   Its not their fault because they physically **lack** that special, extra group of cells in the brain that welcome a questioning conciousness.

   This is definitely Not hereditary.

   It is definitely not their fault.

   ~~They~~ aren't simply misguided.

   Of course the extremes ~~of~~ and levels of the ability to detect injustice range ~~to~~ all levels.

not described these people usually fit in the bracket that
AS Could be ~~easily~~ compared to the level of one who is marginally retarded.

   you know, the ones who have the symptoms of mongoloid rings around the eyes yet they can still act on prime time television dramas.

   All other so called talents like; dance, singing, acting, wood carving and Art is mostly a developmental culmination of exercise ~~trying to attain~~ perfection *thru practice*

   No True talent is ~~or can~~ fully organic.

born  Yet the obviously Superior talented have
passion  not only control of study but that extra special, little gift ⦿ ∞ at birth — fueled by passion. A built in, totally spiritual, unexplainable, New Age, fuckin, cosmic energy bursting love for passion. And yes, they are an even smaller percent amongst the small percent. And they Are Special! mistrust All Systematizers. All things cannot be evaluated to the point of total logic or science. No one is special enough to ~~realize~~ Answer that.

This is not to be taken seriously.
This is not to be read as opinions.
It is to be read as poetry.
Its obvious that I am on the
educated level of about 10th grade in
High school, Its obvious that these
words were not thought out or even
re-read, ~~it's~~ this writing
style is what I like to call thru the perspective
of a 10th grader, her/his attempt at showing that no
matter what level of intelligence one
is on, we all question love and lack
of love and fear of love.
Its good to question authority and to fight it
just to make things a bit less boring,
but ive always reverted back to the the
Conclusion that man is not redeemable
and words that dont necesarily have their
expected meanings can be used descriptively
in a sentence as Art. True english is so
fucking boring. And this little pit-stop
we call life, that we so seriously worry
about is nothing but a small, over the
Week end jail sentence, compared to what
will come with death.
life isn't nearly as sacred as
the appreciation of passion.

*[left margin notes:]* its good
to question
Authority
but The ideas
come to the
same conclusion
that man is
not redeemable
And there
little pit - stop
we call life
that we so
seriously
worry about
is nothing
but A Small
weekend jail
sentence
Compared
to
what will
come with
DEATH

185

If were going to be ghettoised, I'd rather be
in the same slum as bands that are good
like mudhoney, Sonic Youth, the Melvins and Beat happening
rather than being a tennant of the Corporate Landlords
regime.
I mean, were playing the Corporate game and
were playing as best as we can suddenly we
found ourselves having to actually play instead of using the
Corporations great distribution while staying in our little world
because we sold 10 times more the amount of records
we had expected to sell.  It's just a shock
to be doing interviews with magazines that I
don't read

positive>


there are a lot of bands who claim to be alternative
and theyre nothing but stripped down, ex Sunset Strip
hair farming bands of a few years ago
I would love to be erased from our association with
pearl Jam or the Nymphs and other first time offenders.


Alternative bands have tried to          the general public
every year since the sex pistols  and have failed every time
not the fault of the bands but the times weren't right,
the Reagan years were so effective in keeping out too
Any chance of a better concience which is why
there were so many great indie·do it yourself bands throughout
the 80's as suburbs towards Reagan because he was such a
creep.

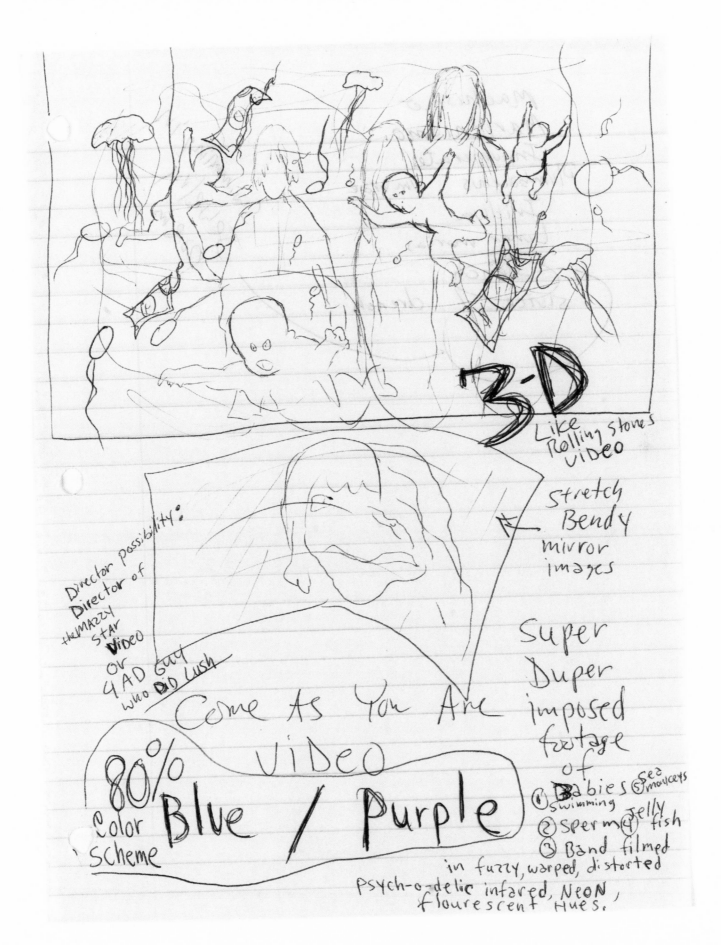

3-D
Like Rolling Stones video

stretch
Bendy
mirror
images

Director possibility:
Director of
the MAZZY
STAR
VIDEO
or
4 AD Guy
who DID LUSH

Come As You Are
video
Blue / Purple

80%
Color
Scheme

Super
Duper
imposed
footage
of
① Babies ⑤ sea monkeys
swimming
② Sperm ④ Jelly fish
③ Band filmed
in fuzzy, warped, distorted
psych-o-delic infared, NEON,
flourescent Hues.

# MELVINS

They have Reagan or Bush vote Republican
stickers on the bumper of their van
to fend off nasty Rodney King Cops

All three members consistently sculpt various models displays
of the Goatee facial hair fashion   oh except for peach fuzz,-
pie eyed, baby face, Sometimes pinch an inchish, sometimes Annorexorcist,
skin tight purple Levis, wearin Jimmy from HR Puffnstuff haircut,
ex-Tea head, Smoking non-smoker   All around nice Guy Dale Crover

oh by
when
has all
that
In the
world

188

Its hard to decipher the difference between
an sincere entertainer and an honest swindler.


Ive ~~vomited~~ violently vomited to the point of
my stomach literally turning itself inside out to show
you the fine hairlike nerves Ive kept and raised
as my children, garnishing and marinating Each one
as if God had fucked me and planted these precious
little eggs, and I parade them around in peacock
victory ~~and~~ maternal pride like a whore relieved
from the duties of repeated rape and torture, promoted to a
more dignified ~~promotion~~ Job of just plain old every day,
good old, wholesome prostitution. my feathers are my pussy.
     CArtoon
oh how I love the brutal effect of just one    offering
word ~~offered~~ to ponder like ....
     Cartoon
fuck man, think about it,
     CArtoon
     HEAVY man
     HEAVY


If you think everythings been said and done
     then how come nothing has been solved
          and resolved?
     I Ask you.
Sarcastically with a sneer. in A 90's way.
     kinda uh, defensively to say the least and to do
                                        the worst.

*kind of*

I feel like a dork writing ~~and do~~ about myself like this as if I were an American pop-Rock Icon - demi God, or

*"A*  self confessed product of corporate-packaged- -rebellion, but Ive heard so many insanely exhaggerated stories or reports from my friends and Ive read so many pathetic second rate, freudian evaluations *from interviews* ~~from my~~ *childhood*

*up until the present state*
*of my →* personality and how ~~I cant handle the success~~ Im A notoriously fucked up Heroine addict, Alcoholic, selfdestructive, yet <u>overtly</u> sensitive frail, fragile, soft spoken, narcoleptic, ~~Auto~~ <u>Neurotic</u>, little piss ant who At any minute is going to O.D. Jump off a roof wig out ~~etc.~~ Blow my head off or All *³ At once* Oh Geez GAWD I cant handle the success! the success! And I feel so incredibly

*Guilt* <u>Guilty!</u> for Abandoning my true commrades
. *the ones who Are devoted.* ~~the ones~~ who were into us A few Years Ago
And ~~After~~ *my In 10 Years* ~~week As~~ *As* memorable As KAJAgoo goo ~~in 10 Years the same~~ *when NIRVANA becomes* *that same,* Very small percent will come to see us At reunion gigs sponsored by Depends diapers, bAld fAt, still trying to RAWK. At ~~water~~ *Amusement* PARKS. *SAturdays* ~~no~~ Puppet show, Rollercoaster & NIRVANA

191

Ask Jenny Tumi if we can re-print her how to record A record essay, for this fanzine.

~~Since~~ After all the hype and oogling over us this past year I've come to two conclusions,
1: we've made A way better commercial record than Poison,
2: there are quadruple the amount of Bad Rock Journalists than there are bad Rock Bands.

Well for those of you who are concerned with my present physical and mental state. I AM NOT A Junkie. I've had a rather unconclusive and uncomfortable stomach condition which by the way is _not_ related to stress which also means it is _not_ an ulcer, because there is no pattern to the burning, nauseas pain in my upper abdominal cavity, I never know when it will ~~come on~~ happen, I can be at home in the most relaxed atmosphere sipping ~~boric acid~~, ~~and~~ & Natural spring water, No stress, No fuss and then WHAM! like A shot gun: stomach time, then I can play 100 ~~shows~~ live performances in A row Guzzle boric Acid & do A zillion television interviews and Not even A Burp. This has left doctors with no ideas except ~~the usual:~~ here Kurt' try another Peptic ulcer pill and let's Jam this fibre optic

(margin note, circled) I AM NOT GAY Although I wish I were, just to piss off Homophobes

(margin note) ~~As say the~~ ~~use~~ perplexed this has left many doctors perplexed

for the past 3 years

tube with a video camera in it down your throat (it's)
[called an endoscope] for the 3rd time and see whats going on in
there Again. yep your in pain alright ice cream from
now on. Your stomach is extremely inflamed and red. try eating
please lord ~~let me have a disease~~ fuck hit
records just let me have my very own unexplainable
rare stomach disease Named After me. ~~And the~~
And the title of our next double Album.
"Cobains disease." ~~the endoscope is great for~~
~~A video and there just about finished with the~~
A rock opera which is all about vomiting Gastric juices
being a borderline Annorexic ~~Auschwitz~~ Auzhwitz - Grunge
- Boy. And with it an accompanying endoscope video. Home-
becoming A vegetarian, exercise, stopping smoking
~~video~~ So After protein drinks and doctors after
doctor I decided to relieve my pain with Heroine small doses of
for A walloping 3 whole weeks. I served as a band-aid for a while
the pain came back so I Quit. It was A but then
stupid thing to do And I'll never do it again and
I feel real sorry for Anyone who thinks they
can use heroine as a medicine because um, duh
it dont work. drug withdrawal is everything
youve ever heard, you puke, you falail around,
you sweat, you shit your bed just like that
movie Christiane F. ~~I don't feel sorry for anyone~~
~~who uses junk.~~ It's evil, leave it alone

I'm not stressed I am the product of 7 months of
I just sit back screaming at the top of my lungs almost every night
and laugh 7 months of jumping around like a retarded wheeusrmonkey
7 months of Answering the same questions over and over
The cherub little scruff you've grown to know from the picture to on the back of Nevermind is
proof that film adds 10 pounds to your body, because I've been the same bird weight
ever since my last excuse which is...

I'm really bored with everyones concerned advice
like: "men you have a really good thing going
your band is great, you write great songs, but
hey man you should get your shit together
personal shit together. Don't freak out
and get healthy. Gee I wish it was as
easy as that but, honestly I didn't want
all this attention but I'm not freaked out
like witch is something a lot of people would like to see
everyone would like to believe. It's
an entertaining thought to our your very
own watch a (Public domain) A Rock figure whos
mentally self destruct, but I'm sorry
friends I'll have to decline. Maybe
Crispin Glover should join our a band.
And at the end of the day, instead of plotting how
I can escape this I find it really funny. I just simply
have to laugh. It feels as if we've
almost, pulled a minor Rock-n-Roll swindle
because I'm not nearly as concerned
with or about myself or anyone
as the media would have us believe
I think the problem with our story is that
there isn't an exciting enough truth for A Good story.
Well I've spewed enough, probably too much
but oh well, for every one self appointed, opinionated,
pissy, self appointed Rock judge Curmudgeon, theres A thousand
kids.

OH THE GUILT    THE GUILT                    (by: KurDt disclaimer-boy)

I kind of feel like a dork writing about the band and myself like
this as if i were an American pop-rock icon, demi god or a self confessed
product of pre packaged, corporate rebellion. But ive heard so many insanely
exhaggerated wise tales and reports from my friends, and ive read so many
pathetic, second rate,freudian evaluations from interviews, regarding
our personalities and especially how im a notoriously fucked up heroine
addict, alcoholic, self destructive, yet overly sensitive,frail,meek,
fragile ,compassionate, soft spoken,narcoleptic, NEUROTIC,little,piss ant
who at any time is going to O.D , jump off a roof and wig out, blow my
head off or all three at once because I CANT HANDLE THE SUCCESS! OH THE
SUCCESS! THE GUILT! THE GUILT! OH, I FEEL SO INCREDIBLY GUILTY! GUILTY
for abandoning our true commrades. the ones who are devoted. the ones
who have been into us since the beginning. the ones who (in ten years
when were as memorable as KAGA GOO GOO)  will still come to see NIRVANA
at reunion gigs at amusement parks. sponsored by depends diapers, bald
fat and still trying to rawk.   MY favorite reocurring piece of advice
from concerned idiots is:"Man, you have a really good thing going.
your band is great.you write pretty good songs and youve sold a shit load
of records but,hey man, you should get your personal shit together. dont
freak out and get healthy." Gee I wish it was that easy but honestly, I
didnt want all this attention, but im not FREAKED OUT!which is something
a lot of people might like to see. Its entertaining to watch A rock figure
whos become public domain mentally self destruct. But im sorry ill have
to decline. Id like to freak out for you . maybe Crispin Glover should
join our band. At the end of the day I laugh my ass offk knowing ive gotten
about 30¢ from this dork. Sometimes it feels as if weve pulled a minor
rock and roll swindle because im not nearly as concerned with or about
myself, the band or anyone as much as the media would like us to believe.
I think the problem with our story is that there isnt an exciting enough
truth for a good story. Oh, and another thing. I am not a heroine addict!
for the past three years ive suffered a rather unconclusive and uncom
fortable stomach condition. which by the way is not related to stress
which also means is not an ulcer because there is no pattern to the burn
ing , nausious pain in my upper abdominal cavity. its like russian roulette,
I never know when it will come on, I can be at home in the most relaxed
atmosphere, sipping natural spring water, no stress, no fuss, and then
wham! like a shot gun.: stomach time is here again.then i can play 100
shows in a row,guzzle boric acid and do a load of television interviews,
results: not even a burp. This has left doctors with no ideas except the
usual, "Here Kurdt, try another peptic ulcer pill and lets jam this fibre-
optic tube  with a video camera on its end down your throat for the third
time.( called an ENDOSCOPE)and see whats going on in there. yep, your in
pain. the stomach lining is extremely red and inflamed. this could be
life threatening. try eating ice cream from now on.  Please lord!
to hell with hit records, let me have my very own unexplainable, rare,
stomach disease named after me. The title of our next double concept album
could be called "COBAINS DISEASE". A rock opera all about vomiting gastric
juices,being a borderline annorexic-Auschwitz-grunge-boy. And with this
epic, an accompanying ENDOSCOPE rock video.
I am the product of seven months of screaming at the top of my lungs almost
every night. seven months of jumping around like a retarded rheesus monkey.
seven months of answering the same questions over and over. The cherub,
little scruff youve grown to know from the back of the nevermind album
is proof that film adds ten pounds to your body, because ive been the same
bird weight since ive had the dreaded gut rot. Well ive spewed enough,
probably too much but oh well. for every one opinionated,pissy,self-appointed
rock judge-cermudgeon, theres a thousand screaming teenagers.
    n hope i die before i turn into Pete Townshend.

195

WomBan

DE_JA VOO- DOO                    BY:  KurDt Kobain

*stomach bile*

An industrial size garbage sack filled with liquid demerol,
sweet cutgrass juice, the urine of extremely retarded,fetal alcohol syn
syndrome victims from Costa Mesa  who are one chromosone away from severely
dangerous examples of why  we will become a third world country in a matter
of years. If this is the current state of the underground,youth culture
Id rather retire to my big mansion petting my pot bellied pig,eating Hagen
Dahs ice cream with this garbage sack I.V. , in an iron lung deprevation
tank,submerged in a glassno no a gold aquarium filled with epsom salts
with full visibility of a television monitor projecting endless footage
of fishing and golfing programs as the grateful dead pumped through
the speaker.  Relaxing , lying naked except for a tie dyed  T- shirt dyed
with the urine of Phil Collins and the blood of Cherry Garcia,
Ill be so relaxed and famous that an old man named Bob will travel miles
to visit me. He will pull apart my pyles and stick it in. He will die
just as he comes inside of me and all of his orgones and bad thoughts
and desires for truth will soak into the walls of my lower intestines.
I will be re-fueled. so re-fueled as to  work up the energy to run on
foot to the grave of Leadbelly, dig up his corpse and put us on a one
way ticket to the Vatican. I will nail the corpse of Huddie in  a corner
of the ceiling, paint him white and decorate him with costume jewelry.


Womben.

Womban

its so relieving to know that your leaving
as soon as you get paid

its so relaxing to know that your asking

its so Soothing to know that youll sue me
whenever you get the chance

its so religious

She eyes me like a pisces – when I am weak
I've been buried in your heart shaped box for weeks
I've been drawn into your magnet tar pit trap
I wish I could eat your cancer when you
    turn black

Hey – wait – I've got a new complaint
 for ever in debt to your priceless advice
Hate – wait – *                          ''

She fries me like cold Ice cream – headaches and chills
                    I'll cook my own Meals

198

uncertainty    certainty

I wish there was someone I could ask for advice,
someone who wouldn't make me feel like a creep
for spilling my guts and trying to explain all
the insecurities that have plagued me for oh, about 25
years now.    I wish someone could explain to me
why exactly I have no desire to learn anymore.
why I used to have so much energy and the need
to search for miles and weeks for anything new
and different. excitement.    I was once a magnet
for attracting new off beat personalities who would
introduce me to music and books that of the
obscure and I would soak it into my system
like a rabid sex crazed junkie hyperactive mentally retarded
toddler who's just had her first taste of sugar.    This weeks
obsession, vagina medical books, the meat puppets and

Lester Bangs

why in the hell do journalists insist
on ~~breading~~ coming up with
a second rate freudian evaluation on my
lyrics when ~~the~~ 90% of the time
they've transcribed ~~the lyrics~~ the lyriss incorectly?

there are more bad Rock journalists than
there are bad Rock bands
~~does anyone remember~~
what the fuck do they teach
journalists at school anyway?
what do they use as
reference or examples?

I would have
printed the lyrics
on the sleeve of
the album if I          does anyone remember lester bangs.
knew it wouldn't    I'm giving you factual quotes from my mind
~~be~~ such          I'm fed up with having a long winded 2 hour
a problem          discussions with journalists and finding ~~they~~
with
people          that they've chosen all the unimportant more
                tabloid esque quotes of the past 2 hours.
                Rock bands are at the mercy of
                the journalist and in my opinion there
                is but one I can think of who deserves
to own a pen.
you probably need more qualifications to
be a welder than ~~a journalist~~ to get
a job being a journalist.

thanks for your second rate freudian
evaluation on my ~~present s~~ minds present
state of "oh gee I feel guilty for
not expecting to sell so many records."

Ask my friends, I've always been this skinny
You know me from pictures, film adds ten pounds
to A person. You've never seen me before in real
life until that most memorable night.

I suffer from narcolepsy, I suffer from
bad sleeping and eating habits, I suffer
from being on tour for 7 fucking months.

Sometimes I wonder if I ~~could~~ could be the very well
luckiest boy in the world.
        For some reason I've been blessed with
loads of neat stuff within the past year and I don't really
think ↓ these baubles and Gifts ~~I have been acquired~~ by
the fact that im a critically acclaimed, internationally
beloved -teen Idol, demi-god like blonde front man,
cryptically honest, Stuttering, Outspoken ~~speech~~ impediment
articulate~~ly~~ award acceptance speech, Golden boy,
    Rock star who has finally, finally
        come out of the closet in regards to his vicious
2 month drug habit, showering the world with ~~a~~ ↑ the
~~utmost~~ Classic I can no longer keep this a
secret because it pains me to hide any part
of my private life from my adoring, concerned,
we think of you as ~~our~~ public domain, cartoon character
but we still love you fans      Yes my children
    in the words of a total fuckin geek ~~who~~ speaking
in behalf of all the world " we really appreciate you
finally admitting what we have been accusing
    you of, we needed to hear it because we were
concerned because the Katty Gossip ~~and~~ Jokes
    and speculation at our jobs schools and parties had
    become well uh, exhausted oh yeah the bitter,
    pissy reincarnation of pick yer king has strayed
    from the positive introduction. so here's the
things I've had the wonderful opportunity to have acquired,
    the wonderful people I've met and the things people
    have said to me that I look back upon and hold dear to my heart.
1st      while in England in ~~the~~ June I went to     Louder
Rough Trade records where I make my pathetic annual,
effort to find the 1st raincoats album

x x x x x x x

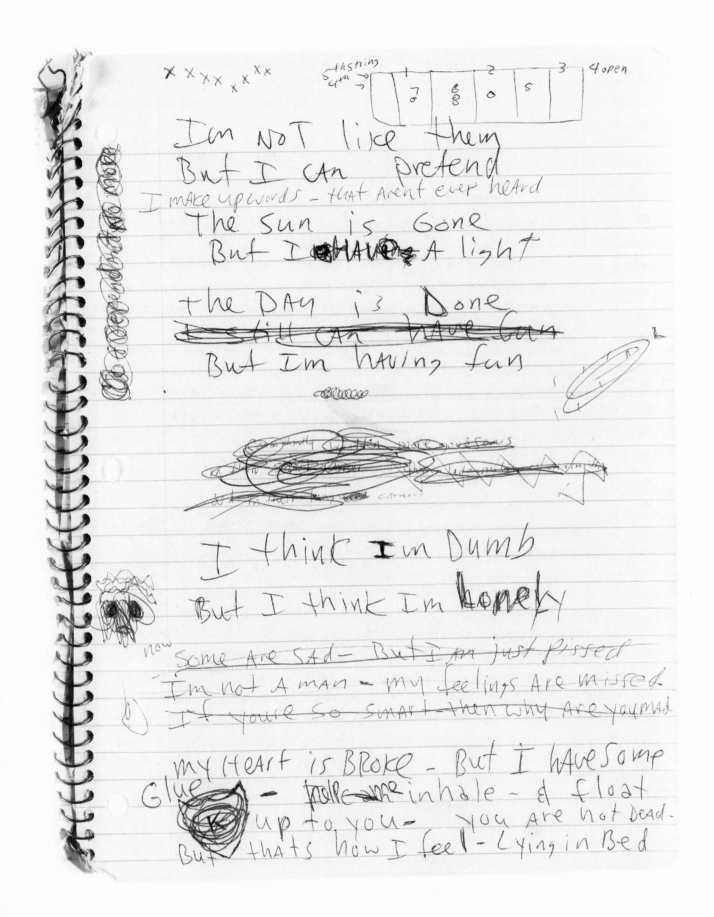

I'm NOT like them
But I can pretend
I make up words - that Aren't ever heard
The Sun is Gone
But I ~~have~~ a light

the DAY is Done
~~I Still can have fun~~
But I'm having fun

I think I'm Dumb

But I think I'm ~~lonely~~

now
~~Some Are SAD - But I'm just pissed~~
~~I'm not A man - my feelings Are missed~~
~~If youre so smart - then why Are you mad~~

my Heart is BRoke - But I have some
Glue - ~~hold me~~ inhale - & float
up to you - you are not Dead.
But thats how I feel - Lying in Bed

I'd be better off if i kept my mouth shut.

But theres a cool breeze chapping my lips
As my jaw hangs open discharging waterfalls
of drool. My eyes are pinned and the stupid
fucking British press bought the lie that I
suffer from narcolepsy.    Yeah, talkin bout
drugs. opening my mouth for the disaffected youth
to ask them a question.   Are you gay?
bisexual? A bigot? A redneck? A prom queen?
A porn star? A topless dancer? did you know the
king, the king of Rockn Roll Elvis presley
died in the bathroom face down, pants down,
choking on blue shag carpet with the remainder
of his stool proudly ~~sticking~~ sticking out of his
big fat Ass?   Are you kinda mad sometimes
At your mom or dad kinda, in a way?
         I went on, A three week Heroine
    Binge after our last European tour, got a little
habit, Kicked it in A Hotel in three days ( sleeping
Killing, vomiting and the worst gas youll ever
know. then 3 days later ~~Ive~~ we went on A
Australian tour ~~And on~~ to Japan during which I
collected a very distressing stomach disorder,
went to A doctor and he gave me stomach
pills that Ive had before and didn't work and
some five milligram methadone tablets.
    They stopped the stomach pains, I ran out
when I got home then went to A hospital
for a few days to recover from that.
    More bad gas.

~~Roth I don't do drugs anymore~~
Yeah, I went on A 3 week drug binge and now
I'm thought of ~~As an~~ emaciated, yellow skinned, Zombie like-
~ Evil drug fiend, Junky, ~~drugs~~ lost cause, on the
brink of Death, Self destructive, selfish Pig,
A loser who shoots up in the back stage ~~area~~ just seconds before
~~going on~~ a performance

I tried heroine the first time in 1987 in aberdeen and proceeded to use it about 10 more times from 87 to 90. when I got back from our second European Tour with Sonic Youth I decided to use heroine on a daily basis because of an ongoing stomach ailment that I had been suffering from for the past five years had literally taken me to the point of wanting to kill myself. For five years every single day of my life. Every time I swallowed a piece of food I would experience an excruciating burning nauseous pain in the upper part of my stomach lining. The pain became even more severe on tour due to lack of a proper and regimented eating schedule and diet. Since the beginning of this disorder Ive had 10 upper and lower Gastrointestinal proceedures wich found an enflamed irritation in the same place. I consulted 15 different doctors and tried about 50 different types of ulcer medication. The only thing I found that worked were heavy opiates. There were many times that I found myself literally incapacitated in bed for weeks vomiting and starving. So I decided I feel like a junky as it is so I may as well be one. After the last European tour I vowed to never go on tour again unless my condition is either masked or cured. I did heroine for about one month then found myself realizing that I wouldnt be able to get drugs when we go to Australia and Japan so Courtny and I detoxed in a Hotel room

I went to Australia and of course the stomach pain started immediately. We had to cancel A few shows because the pain left me immobile doubled up on the bathroom floor vomiting water and blood. I was literally starving to death. my weight was down to about 110 lbs. I was taken to a doctor at the advice of my management who gave me physeptone. ~~take methadone~~ The pills seemed to work better than anything else I've tried a bit later into the tour I read the fine print on the bottle it read: "physeptone - contains methadone!" Hooked again. We survived Japan but by that time opiates and touring had started to take their toll on my body. and I wasn't in much better health than I was off of drugs. I returned home to find that country had gotten hooked again so we checked ~~her~~ into a detox center for 2 weeks. She recovered. I instantly regained that familiar burning nausea and decided to ~~either~~ kill myself or ~~to~~ stop the pain. I bought a gun but chose drugs instead. I stayed on heroine until one month before frances due date. again I checked into a detox center and went through 2 months of the slowest process I have ever witnessed in recovery 60 days of starvation and vomiting. Hooked to an IV and moaning out loud with the worst stomach pain I have ever experienced. ~~B~~ by the last 2 weeks I was introduced to a medicine called buprenorphine which I found eleviates the pain within minutes. It has been used experimentally in A few detox centers for opiate and cocaine withdrawal. the best thing about it is that there are no known side effects. ~~and~~ It acts ask an opiate but it doesn't get you high. I've been on an increasingly smaller dose of it for nine months and haven't had a single stomach episode since. The potency range of beprenorphine is that like a mild barbiturate on a scale of 1 to 10 its a 1 and heroine i's 10. of

Dear Empty TV
the Entity of all corporate
GODS.

how fucking dare you embrace
such trash journalism from an
overweight, unpopular at high school,
Cow who severely needs her karma
Broken. My lifes Dedication
is NOW TO DO Nothing
But SLAG MTV and
LYNN Herschberg

who by the way is in Kahoots with
her lover Kurt Loder (Gin blossom drunk)!

We will survie without

you. easily
the old school is going

DOWN FAST

Kurdt
Kobain
professional
Rock musician         FUCK FACE

# 4 month media blackout

use just once and destroy
invasion of our piracy
after birth of a nation
starve without your skeleton key

(3) ✗ I love you for what I am not
    ✗ I did not want what I have got
(4) ✗ blanket ached with cigarette burns
    speak at once while taking turns

(1) ✗ this has nothing to do with what you think
    ✗ If you ever think at all
    ~~who's capros the flow~~
    ~~revolutionary debris~~
    ~~litters the floor of wall street~~

what is what I need — what is wrong with me
what is what I need — what do I think I
think

we use your enemies              Bridge ☆
and save save your friends
and find find your place
and spit spit the truth

(2) ✗ Bi polar opposites attract
    ✗ All of a sudden my water broke
    ~~free xeroxes~~ for all alternateens
(3) ✗ second rate word by pass throat
                    of ferns

Hes such a knob

# 9 month media
# BLACKout

I love you my lovely dear
I dont want you any where

I want you to be my bride
no not really, I just lied

Will you love me **with** your might
I'll beat you an inch ↑from your life
                        AWAY

hold me tight with breaths of truths
I wish a terminal disease on you

Gosh I feel so darn confused
ever felt like youve been used?

Bi-polar opposites attract

All of a sudden my water broke

I love you for what I'm not

primary
  ↳ second rate word play bypass throat throat

Bypass  Use once and destroy
        invasion of our piracy
        afterbirth of a nation
        blanket acned with cigarette
        I forget what I look like to you burns

        starve without your skeleton key

A matter of opinion

# Personal Preference

A Date With FUSION

Raw Power
Funhouse } the Stooges
the Stooges

Generic Flipper — Flipper

Surfer Rosa — Pixies

Trompe le Monde — Pixies

Pod — Breeders

VAselines pink EP

Aerosmith — Rocks

Gang of four — entertainment

Nevermind the Bullocks — Sex pistols

Flowers of Romance — PIL

Jamboree — Beat Happening

Superfuzz Big Muff — Mudhoney

Leadbellys lAst session — Hudie Ledbetter

LAnd shark — Fang

Millions of dead cops — MDC

Damaged — Black flag

Scratch acid EP — scratch acid

Locust abortion Technician — butthole surfers

Rock for light — Bad Brains

Raincoats — Raincoats

Philosophy of the World — shaggs

Combat Rock — clash

Are we not men — Devo

B-52s

Collosal Youth — Young Marble Giants

Kleenex

Slits — Slits

Daydream Nation — Sonic Youth

man who Sold the world — David Bowie

GI — Germs

Saccharine Trust — EP

Get the knack — the knack

Atomizer — Big black

Great expectations — Jad fair

Is this Real ⟩ wipers

Youth of America

Rubbing the impossible to burst — Hussy Bear

XTC

Jackie 362 9610

**M. Carrodus—**
**"Squadron Formation**
**King."**
**TEBALA MOTORCYCLE CORPS**
**TEBALA TEMPLE A A O N M S**
**Rockford, Illinois**
This unit participates in Shrine and Civic Parades.
Performs in Precision Maneuvers

Tel. (415) 986-8866

1441 Grant, San Francisco, CA 94133

QP 549

Hi Ian and Nikki,
Happy New year, merry Xmas
Happy Halloween, Happy Valentines
day, Happy Thanksgiving,
HAPPY Birthday, maybe
sometime next year I could
squeeze my friends into my
Rock-schedule and we all
could go shriner Bowling.
Love Kurdt

QUANTITY POSTCARDS
Mfr./Pub./Wholesale/Retail/Mail Order

Catalogue
available

©1987 Quantity Postcards

213

SWINGERS

ALICIA OSTRIKER

Passing that fiery tree—if only she could

Be making love,
Be making poetry,
Be exploding, be speeding through the univers

Like a photon, like a shower
Of yellow blazes—7

214

Flipper

washed up, has been, drug addicts.

**70 sheets/college ruled**
**11x8½in/27.9x21.6cm**

~~the~~ barium never left me
Cigarette burns in Comforters
riddled with approach
   Cursed ~~with~~ welcome talents
Ive never been so yes


I know exactly what im doing
its all under control
   I dont need any help
   Id rather not
   please leave me be
Control freak
I appreciate your concern
   has gratuity been added?
      Set it down over there
      ~~officer handler~~
      handler of the gods

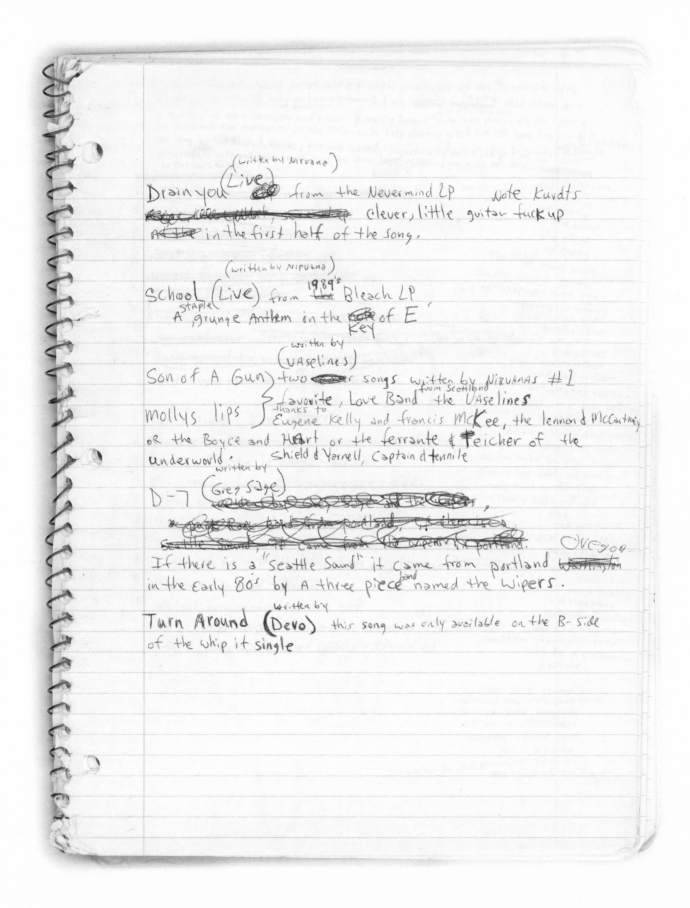

(written by Nirvana)

Drain you (Live) from the Nevermind LP    note Kurdts
clever, little guitar fuckup
in the first half of the song.

(written by Nirvana)

School (Live) from 1989's Bleach LP
staple
A grunge Anthem in the Key of E

written by
(Vaselines)

Son of A Gun) two songs written by Nirvanas #1
} favorite, Love Band from Scotland the Vaselines
thanks to
Mollys lips    Eugene Kelly and francis McKee, the lennon & McCartney
or the Boyce and Hart or the ferrante & Teicher of the
underworld. Shield & Yarnell, Captain & tennile
written by

D-7 (Greg Sage)

If there is a "Seattle Sound" it came from portland Oregon
in the Early 80's by A three piece band named the Wipers.

written by
Turn Around (Devo) this song was only available on the B-side
of the whip it single

ℓ

Additional Cut
for a jaguar
wing.

Slimmed
left wing

Slimmed and
reshaped
right body

extended
Butt
on left
side

This is a mustang ~~cut~~ cut differently
with a few inches added to the wing
and left side of butt and the left
wing and side cut thinner

mustang/Jaguar
Jagstang
**LEFT HANDED**

Color:
Aqua blue/green

very thin neck
small fret
wire

mustang single
coils
& electronics

white tortoise
shell pickGuard

Double coil
pickup

whatever
bridge & tailpiece
works best

Tune-o-matic
Bridge

Hot double coil
bridge Pickup

Not sure what kind yet

Probably sg Les Paul

Dots

Arched
Headstock

Jaguar
Front Pickup

or just A simple
Jaguar neck
and Headstock

Schaller
tuners

mustang pickup

Hot Rail

3 - way
pickup
push button

Vol

Tone

Humbucker

Color: Same old blue/green/aqua
from the mustang

Convexed
Curve on
Back

preferably jaguar tailpiece
and tune o matic bridge
or whatever is simplest

mustang guts switches

Jaguar front
Pick up

cream colored
tortoise shell

double coil
Pickup
Preferably Sq'lespaul

If this Headstock isnt possible,
then the old fender headstock will
be fine!

LEFT HANDED!®

Kurt Kobain model
1993

c/o gold Mountain ent
Cahuenga blvd  west
Suite 450 LACA 90068

michael meisel / John Silva

223

with the phrasing I Allow myself it isn't ~~very~~ easy to
be ~~used~~ lyrically prolific

~~I like Girls~~

Boys write Songs for Girls - what a simple world
how the hell do I - Know whats on inside
what else should I SAy? - All my words Are grey
what else could I write? - I'm sorry I am white

Such an eAsy thing - such a shiny ring
let me grow some breAsts - I cheated on my test
I dont have ~~the~~ right - to sAy whats on your mind
your not allowed to sing - All Apologies

In the sun in the sun I feel As one in the sun
in the sun I'm married and buried

you have every right - to want to start a fight
~~treated like a dog~~
~~its gone on too long - treated like their dogs~~
~~such an easy thing - let~~ my sister sing
what else can I do? - I'm in love with you

Seven months ago I chose to put myself in a position which requires the highest form of responsibility a person can have. A responsibility ~~of which control~~ that should not be dictated ~~by thinking that I should rather want~~ to take on this responsibility. ~~Every~~ Everytime I see a television show that has dying children or seeing a testimonial by a parent who recently lost their child I can't help but cry. The thought of losing my baby haunts me every day.

I'm even a bit unnerved to take her in the car in fear of getting into an accident. I swear that If I ever find myself in a similar situation than you've ~~been in it~~ the divorce I will fight to ~~my~~ death to keep the right to provide for my child. I'll go out of my way to remind her that I love her more ~~than~~ I love myself. not because it's a fathers duty but because I want to out of love. And If Courtney and I end up hating eachothers guts we both will be adult and responsible enough to be pleasant to one another when our child is around us.

I know ~~that~~ you've felt for years that my mother has somehow brainwashed Kim and I into hating you, ~~which~~ I can't stress enough how totally untrue this is and I think it's a very lazy and lame excuse to use for not trying harder to provide your fatterly duties. I can't recall my mother ever talking shit about you until much later in the game, right around the last two years of High school. That was a time when I came to my own realizations without the need of my mothers input. Yet she ~~let the~~ noticed my contempt for you and your family and acted upon my feelings in accordance by taking the opportunity to vent her ~~frustrations~~ out on you. Every time she talked shit about you I've let her know that I don't appreciate it and how unnecessary I think it is. I've never taken sides with you or my mother because while I was growing up I had equal contempt for you both.

# MR Producer

*try to find oak or maple sheets to be nailed on rough plywood*

UTENCILS: five 5ft × 5ft pieces of plywood. thickness depends on type of wood. preferrably ½ inch thick. Carpeted on one side each. Thick, dense carpet is preferred.

<u>Guitar</u>: RCA ribbon mics

looking for a transducer element

<u>Beyer</u> 160 - 130      BK-5 ?

With <u>Beyer</u> 4 to 6 inches close to amp. no closer or static breakage will result.

<u>Setting:</u> the closer to the cabinet the bassier with most other brands.

Amp Settings: ① try mids on full.
② try Highs at lower than usual setting.
③ Lows full.

④ Use carpeted Cabinet.
⑤ build or use A large cardboard box for muffle chamber, or pieces of plywood with carpet to make an enclosure around the cabinet. allowing at least 2 feet of breathing space

EFFects: slight Compression.
Room chamber
Alessis very small dimensions

carpeted Plywood

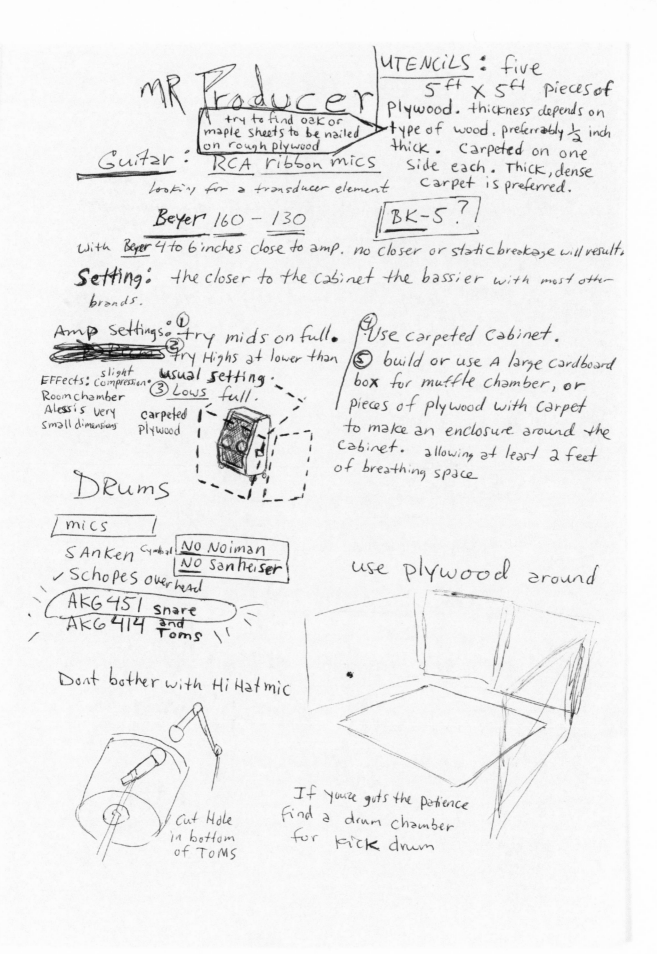

# DRums

<u>mics</u>

Sanken  Cymbal  NO Noiman
✓ Schopes overhead  NO Sanheiser

AKG 451 snare
AKG 414 and Toms

Dont bother with Hi Hat mic

use plywood around

Cut Hole in bottom of TOMS

If youre gots the patience find a drum chamber for kick drum

# New ideas
## for Mevins

put mics inside Toms

record dale with cymbals
Heavily taped so they make
No Noise! this will allow us
to use the room mics A lot louder
then dub cymbal§ crashes later.

put three mics on the snare
one of them will be recorded
Very Very hot to the point of

distortion After about 4 dbs

And 2 more room mics
besides the little scraper room
mics About 3 feet Away
from kick And snares

more chorus on Bass guitar.

use very directional mics for this

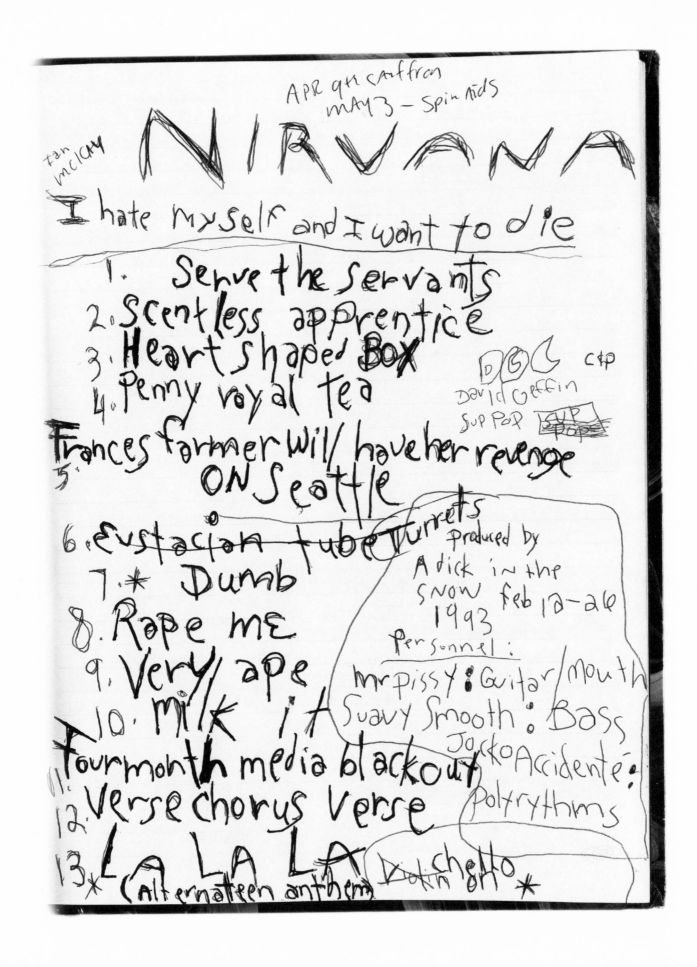

APR 9th cancfrom
MAY 3 — Spin Aids

Ian McClay

# NIRVANA

I hate myself and I want to die

1.  Serve the servants
2. Scentless apprentice
3. Heart shaped Box
4. Penny royal tea

David Geffin
DGC C$P
Sup Pop  SUP POP

Frances farmer will have her revenge
5.  ON Seattle

6. Eustacian tube Turrets
7. * Dumb
8. Rape me
9. Very ape
10. Milk it
11. Four month media blackout
12. Verse chorus verse
13. * LA LA LA (Alternateen anthem) Doin ghetto *

Produced by
A dick in the
Snow feb 12-26
1993
Personnel:
Mr Pissy : Guitar/mouth
Suavy Smooth : Bass
Jocko Accidente :
Polyrhythms

230

Hi Simon,
Thanks a load for the
drawings, pictures and music,
They're the best presents I've ~~gotten~~ recieved
in a really long time!
I looove the stinky
puffs! and would love to hear
more once you all record some
more. I was wondering if
you would be interested in drawing
some pictures for the cover of
the next NIRVANA record wich will
be ready to sell once we have the
artwork done. I think you draw
really good and ——→ (over)

It would mean a lot to me if you'd consider it. heres some ideas I had.

NIRVANA

I hate myself and I want to die

DAVE ← or → chris n kurt

WHATEVER YOU WANT

It would be great if you drew about 5 or more or less so we have plenty to choose between.

the title of the album is rather negative but kind of funny. Its called:

I hate myself and I want to die.

Heres some info that needs to be written for the back of the LP
DAVE-drums. chris-bass. kurt Geetar-n-mouth.
D.G.C records and subpop. recorded by steve albini.
Cello on LALALA & dumb oh, and Artwork
by simon Timony   well, bye  write back soon
love kurdt. Hi Jad! &

Since my freshly found relationships with employees of the *corporate ogre* ~~example~~ *(catch phrase © copyright Calvin Johnson of Beat Happening)* I've ~~found~~ ~~restad~~ learned that there are a handful of very honorable and sincere ~~p~~ music lovers who are posing as the enemy to infiltrate the mechanics of the empire. to help destroy what we all have known for too long as ~~bullshit~~ shit Rock, prefabricated, incestually politically business; oriented garbage a smoke screen, honesty and true talent and to keep ~~the will~~ having to kiss ass or risk ~~the no~~ using a to clog the arteries of those unchallenging, and most importantly undeserving at the top of the Heap.

the Heap of Dung.

The Heap ~~it~~ starts with the Ass kissers ~~to~~ all the way up to the top where the cherry or music publication sits old school looking down on the Baby Birds with eyes still shut, and feeding them dehydrated worms. But As I said before the small percent of deserving bands and music loving employees will keep sawing away at the Heap and if we fail we will just simply wait until the cherry rots of old Age and we will use your Historical decomposition as a reference or a sweaty bed time story As remembrance of a warning to next time, plant our seeds closer to a cleaner Asshole.

1. ~~Sonic Youth~~ ~~Goo~~
2. ~~Every good boy deserves fudge — Mudhoney~~
3. ~~Bandwagonesque — Teenage Fanclub~~
4. ~~Trompe Le Monde — Pixies~~
5. ~~Beat Happening — dreamy~~
X 6. ~~Violent Femmes — Why do birds sing?~~
X 7. ~~Bull Head — Melvins~~
8. ~~Strangely Beautiful EP Television personalities~~
9. ~~Army of Lovers — Pretty little Baka Guy reissue — Shonen Knife~~
10. ~~Bleach out of time Hole — pretty on inside~~
~~No 1 single — crucified — Army of Lovers~~

1  Sonic youth — Goo — DGC
2  Mudhoney — Every good boy deserves fudge — Sub Pop
3  Pixies — Trompe le Monde — Elektra
4  Teen age fanclub — Bandwagonesque — DGC
5  Hole — pretty on the inside — Karoline
6  Beat Happening — dreamy — Sub Pop
7  Television personalities — strangely beautiful EP — Fire records
8  Shonen Knife — Pretty little Baka Guy (reissue) Zero (Japanese import)
9  Melvins — Bullhead — Boner
10 Violent femmes — why do birds sing?

P.S. Urge Overkill — Supersonic storybook — Touch-n-Go
NO 1 Single: Army of Lovers — Crucified

You have ~~failed~~ at conditioning the young ones of the underworld whom you have spawned, and you yourselves ~~are~~ ~~seated~~ should have been Kleenex or poached fried or scrambled sperm, ~~or~~ neutered eggs.

233

Serve the servants

Initially this song was about coming of age during a time where your old enough to support yourself without the aid of your parents. A theme for the twenty somethings, if you will not. Ive always felt that a person doesnt necessarily have to force themselves to love their parents simply because of blood. If you dont like your parents or relatives, dont fake it tell them how you feel and in my own way I decided to let my father know that I dont hate him. I simply dont have anything to say and I dont need a father son relationship with a person whom I dont want to spend Christmas with. In other words; I love you. I dont hate you. I dont want to talk to you.

A Boring

Scentless apprentice

~~what about report?~~ ~~~~ "perfume" by Patrick Susskind

Heart shaped box                                    ~~revised~~

Camille's ~~flower/vagina theory~~ vaginal/flower theory bleeding and spreading into ~~fabric~~ the fabric that leonardo would have used to ~~revise the~~ improve ~~the his~~ hang glider but he died before he could change the course of history. shit. I Claudius I play dumb for thee! and dorothy and toto (the dog) not the band. and rusty pyles. ~~The fem~~ The male seahorse empragnates the female seahorse, she ~~carries the~~ holds them through most of the developmental stages then transferes the babies to the father who carries them through the last stages ~~then~~ and finally gives them birth. ~~They share~~ ~~~~ ~~transformation~~

The majority of our so called Outlaw heroes of the old west were nothing but fucked up psychopath ~~sympathisers ex~~ Confederate soldiers. Sympathisers of the way it used to be with alcohol fuled Bi polar ~~internal~~ rage during the transformation years. killing every darkie they could find. Heroes my ass! ~~~~ If I only had a heart. ~~I dont~~ listen you snivelling little, opinionated, spoiled punts, H I dont hate you. I love you. Ah god it feels so good to be clean DR Bronner.

Kinda like when Axl ~~~~ was butt neked in that epic video of his.

## Rape me

How Bold ~~should the print be~~ shall ~~I make the print~~ ~~the print be made?~~

~~In order to help you in the simple process of Reading?~~
~~Please don't question~~

OBvious. oblivious. settle down. calm. calm. its ok. sshh.
Hold still. Sshh. Hold still.

## Frances farmer will have her revense on Seattle.

The conspirators are still alive and well in their comfortable, warm, safe home's.
gag on her ashes. gag on her gash. uh, god is ~~so~~ A woman and she's
~~Black~~ . BACK in Black

## Dumb

All that pot. all that supposedly unaddictive, harmless, safe
reefer that damaged my nerves and ruined my memory and made
me feel like wanting to ~~kill~~ blow up the prom. and the patience
to play guitar for 5 hours every day after school. and to sleep
during the day when I should have paid a bit more attention
to my studies. especially in English sometimes an At sometimes
an X on my hand or forehead and the feeling that it just
wasn't ever strong enough so I climbed the ladder to the
poppie. Not everyone does the latter so I've learned one lesson,
I have absolutely no right to express my opinions until I
know all the answers. far out.

## Very ape

I forget.

## penny royal tea

An ~~abortive~~ herbal abortive.
'it doesn't work you hippie.'

## Radio friendly Unit shifter

Boy this will really get the A&R mans Bloodboiling.
Héll be so Pissed. heh heh. Clever.
. getting into the inner me. self indulgent.
way out there ~~idea~~.
~~the to play live~~

Ask about Dantes Inferno movie from the 30's
to use instead of making our own props
we will use the scenes of people intwined old withering oak trees

Sebadoh

Alex wages

tourrets

me. old man. ~~have made~~
have made my conclusion. but nobody will listen any more.

Birds. Birds are and always have been reincarnated old men
with tourrets syndrome ~~and every morning~~ having somehow managed
to ~~earn~~ the reproductive saga ~~and~~ they fuck eachother and
dupe
tend to their home repairs and children. while never missing
their true mission. to scream at the top of their lungs
in horrified hellish rage every morning at day break
to warn us all of the truth. they know the truth.
screaming bloody. murder all over the world in our ears
but sadly we dont speak bird.
the whales respond i~~n a similar way~~ with their message for
us in similar ways. by beaching themselves

this album is dedicated to dead relatives.
they are warm and full of happy smiles.
SAfe

## All apologies

Nothing has or will
Nothing could or should
Alternateens ignoring the Budweiser sponsor banner behind the 10 yrs + acts.
An excuse to get laid

~~Kurt loder and tabitha soren are completely~~

Jimmy Carter was ~~great~~ and still is an extremely loving and sensible man. but when I was a kid I only remember that he liked peanuts and had big lips.

## milk it

If you really love me you will send medical supplies.

oh god. he's awake again. don't look. just ignore it. before he starts to. oh shh. he fell asleep again. thank God.
How do you feel? Shhh be quiet.

A multitude
## serve ~~the~~ servants

Oh lord the guilt of sucksess. ~~during~~ during the past two years I have slowly come to the conclusion that I do not want to die. ~~now~~ I am now no more of a recluse than I used to be. I lived in the Ⓚ kingdom for a few years hiding in a little apartment. ~~and it~~ And now I stand in my room without a sendbox ~~so I dont offer~~ on punk rock show attendent ratio I would say it's about the same. I am still equally annoyed and equally impressed with the same old familiar ritual of standing in a room full of people hoping to feel a vibration that runs through my back when I hear a familiar song or see an enigmatic performance from ~~so~~ ~~a few~~ a which are electrically activated and manipulated who choose to strap on pieces of wood which are electrically activated and manipulated I've never claimed to be a punk rocker.

I was inspired by it. as much as led zeppelin or Aerosmith

237

& the beatles etc. but oh lord never paul pleeeease!
Is it egotistical to talk about myself like this?
I guess this song is for my father who is incapable of
communicating at a level of affection in which I have always
expected

Nordic trAc
1-800 382 9177

Aygment ensamble

verile

Keular

Kevin & Co
　　　　for the Long form

~~On Anurysm~~

~~On Anurysm: keep the Audio from the Amsterdam show but keep~~
~~the edits from out the same~~

1  ON Anurysm: Keep Amsterdam audio when first change happens ie. kurdt in over coat

2  Take out Dave & Chris playin Aerosmith song

3  Put Subtitle in " Bronchitis " flashing throughout Dive

4  Video ~~footage~~ of us with Jason "the early years) put in sub title = Jason everman guitar Chad channing drums Rhino Records LA 88. Song. Sifting

5　　Cut out the last half of dave talking about new bands

6　　Start my rant just as I say Black flag flipper ~~the finish~~ ~~the rest~~ leave the rest.

Sub 7  Rock-star lesson: ~~sing out of tune your guitar is~~
title  (for Come As U are)  when your guitar is out of tune, sing out of tune along with it

~~The ~~

8  Englands prestigious Top of the pops equivalent of US's American Bandstand.

Cut to 1st IN Bloom video we did with one camera in dresses destroying the set.

9  Replace mollys lips with Reading version with ~~Eugene~~ Eugene singing

Add the scene where I hand the guitar to the audience. I think its from Reading

And the    penis and flower petal
face in camera ~~the~~ performance
piece kurdt does in Rio.

~~the first Vinyl Relm~~
but the video's recorded Audio version will
be ~~the~~ re-mixed one.

---

① release Albini version: <u>mastered</u> - different sequence under <u>title</u>:
~~I Hate myself and want to die~~
on Vinyl LP, Cassette and <u>8-track</u> ← Yes! Yes! Yes!
Albini producer, mixologist credits. with sticker that says: NIRVANAS
Latest studio release for 93' contains Heart shaped box, Rape me & 12 others.
<u>Retail</u>: Sold to small mom and pop stores or anywhere Vinyl can be found.
NO - PROMOS sent out !!!
② one month later: after many lame reviews and reports
on the curmudgeonly, uncompromising Vinyl, cass, 8-track only release.
we Release the Re-mixed ~~version~~ & re-recorded ~~at~~ bass and Acoustic
guitar version under the title: "Verse Chorus Verse" on Vinyl LP, cassette,
and God forbid, Cd. with <u>sticker</u> that says: This Album is the radio-
friendly, unit shifting, compromise version which, by the way, NIRVANA is
extremely proud of. contains Heart shaped box, Rape me & 10 more.
③ Release Video of Heart shaped box at the same time of the 1st
Vinyl, cass, 8-track only release. but the re-mix audio version will accompany
it.

Hi, im the moody, bohemian member
of the group.            blonde frontman.
the sensetive artist type.

I like: pasta, turtles, girls with weird eyes,
writing, reading, keeping my mouth shut,
cake decorating, horseback riding, gun cleaning,
Sally Struthers impersonations, pina coladas
and getting caught in the rain, buttfucking,
accupuncture, painting, friends, cats, goats,
mo-hair sweaters, cultivating a fine army of
facial blemishes, scarification, playing music with
my band, my ~~girlfriend~~ wife, ~~and~~ my family and all of
the people with whom our band works with.

I would only wear a tie died T shirt if it were made from the
and the urine of phil Collins. Blood of Gerry Garcia

shocking Blue
wire,                    the vaselines, the breeders, the Stooges, the pixies, Sexpistols,

Here Are
Some of the              raincoats, melvins, tales of terror, scratch acid, butthole surfers,
BANDS I
like.

Leonard cohen,           young marble giants, urge overkill, marine girls, Jesus lizard, fanclub Teenage

Pylon B-52's             slits, mudhoney, Beat happening, cramps, Shonen knife, Delta 5

Duh, Didjits             Sonic youth, Black flag, R.e.m, meat puppets II, witchy poo, Hole,

Mazzy star,              TV personalities, Daniel Johnston, the Sonics, lead belly, the wipers,

Sun city girls  ⟨TK records⟩   Half Japanese, Dead moon, public enemy, Big Black, ~~the knack~~, Germs,
                 sprinkler

Calamity Jane            Husker Du, Dinosaur Jr, Captain America, saints, velvet underground,

Tinklers, some
velvet sidewalk          Lee Hazlewood, Hank williams, flipper, feederz, Lewd, Bad Brains,
          Smegma
          Go team        Patsy Cline, Devo, Clash, ~~Devo~~ Fear, Army of Lovers,

Rites of spring          fugazi, ~~⬤⬤⬤⬤⬤~~ Bikini Kill, ~~⬤⬤⬤⬤⬤⬤⬤~~

void shop
    Assistants           Beatnik Termites, the staple singers, Discharge, Cannanes, Bratmobile, Saccharine trust,
Nip Drivers,             Dirt, pavement, love child, Superchunk, Boredoms, Sebadoh, Axemen, Cows  →

(Fire records)
339 seven sisters RD          Suck dog
London N15 6rd England     PoBx 1491 Dover NH, 03820     (AK48)
                                                          Simple machines
independent labels ~~address~~       PO Box 10290 Arlington VA
                              90260                    22210-1290
SST: Po box 1 Lawndale CA K  Seminal twang
    25520 Chicago IL 60625  Box Olympia WA
Touch and Go              7154  K  98507  Sympathy for the record industry
                          Bo
Boner, matador, **Sub pop**,  ecstatic peace   CASATANKA
                                                           Rockville
Kill rock stars, feel good all over, Homestead 4-AD
Rough Trade Caroline C/D presents  T/K records  Alternative
out of        114 West 26th St                            Tentacles
Business     NY, NY 10001      42423 Portland Oregon
music publications;  fact sheet five.     97242    Twin Tone
CAll                FANZINES;  Bikini kill  Alternative    Jigsaw  INK Disease
Thurston                                  press                    Your flesh
    Girl germs, flip side, maximum Rock n roll
murder can be fun, Spin, forced exposure,
Amok Research, Option, Kitten Kore, And she's not even pretty.

Technicolor effect for film.

Old weathered man in hospital bed with a rubber foetus
in his IV Bottle chris dave and I sitting at the foot of
the bed, impatiently waiting for him to pass away. In the hospital
room the curtains are drawn 90% of the way with a blinding white
light shooting through the curtains. Lots of flowers in the room
and kurdt hold an old pocket watch dangling back and forth—
indicating that time is running out.

4 year old aryan girl with bright blonde hair with vivid blue eyes.
in a klu klux klan robe on sitting in a small shack.
the walls of the shack is covered with stargazer lillies with stems cut
off and the butt end of the flowers and glued on the every where on the
walls. Each flower has a bright light alluminating each of them.
from behind them. another shot of the little girl holding hands with
an elder. he squeezes her hand as if she could never escape.
bright red blood soaks in from inside of the girls robe.
Close up of red ink or blood soaking in to white fabric
then a gust of wind blows her lekk hat off, the camera follows it
through blowing above a field of poppies. eventually the hat turns
into a butterfly net and chases butterflies through out the field.
then it falls into a small pool of black tar ( india ink.
another close up of black ink-goo soaks into the white fabric.
then we see after the hat is completely black it appears to be
a black witches hat and blows away bat with a gust of wind.

~~Old men on a cross~~
Old weathered interesting looking man on a cross with black crows
on his arms, pecking at his face — Scarecrow/Jesus.

Animation, forest Dantes inferno from the thirties
Bodies entwined in old oak trees
maybe we can use the original
footage from that movie

Optical illusion

Your All absolutely one hundred percent correct.
I was severely wrong when I wrote "For me
Punk Rock is dead. although it is dead
for me which were the key words I wrote
in those oh so negative and retarded linear
notes. The ~~two~~ words for was miss printed
at the ~~the~~ printing offices when they translated
my handwriting. ~~Instead~~ The word to was
used instead of for which is a very common
occurance when deadlines are due and
people are scratching like mexican fighting cocks
to get an approval for something as non important
as ~~a~~ liner notes to a B- side cash cow.
  Yes friends. punk rock is dead for me.

Letter to the Editor.
I thought I would let the
world know how much I
Love ~~them~~ people. I thought
I would ~~make art~~ try to create something that
I would personally like to listen to.
because a very large portion
of this worlds art sucks
beyond description. ~~But~~ yet I
~~Besides~~, feel that, It's a waste of
time to pass judgement. and
who the fuck am I to
declare myself an authority who's
certified, one who has the
right to critique. I guess
in a way anyone with enough
ambition to create and not
take away is someone who

deserves respect. There are
~~those~~ who are better at it than
others. there are some who
have severely large amounts
of enthusiasm who are prolific
as Hell, spewing out a million
products a year. Yeah products.
they are ones who usually give
10% good and 90% crap.
Then there are those who spend
years studying other peoples
works because they dont have
a chance in Hell to produce
anything with a hint of talent.
Yeah talent. But like I
said no one should be denied
the priviledge to create
and some people most

Certainly do not need the
fear of whether their goods
are better or worse
than the Best or worse.
They can find that out for
themselves.
                        maybe I
On second thought ~~I thought~~
~~I would~~ just tried to let the world
know how much I love
myself. like a hypocrite
in a hippie crypt.
      I hate myself and I
want to die
      Leave me alone.
           Love Kurdt

Love Child – He's So sensitive
Love Child – Diane
Calamity Jane – Car
Beatnik Termites – when she's nearby
Sun City Girls – **Voice of America #1**
Discharge – The more I see
Jadfair – the Crow
Jadfair – take a chance
Jadfair – I like Candy
Mazzy Star – Halah
Didjits – under the Christmas fish
Bags – Babylonian Gorgon
Bags – Survive
Bags – We will bury You
**Sebadoh – Loser Core**
Duh – spaghetti and red wine
TV Personalities – I know where Syd Barret lives
Axemen – mourning of Youth

Side 2
Daniel Johnston
Continues stories
**StinkyPuffs** – stinky Puffs theme
Hamburger
How You make A car
Baby A monster

Courtney, when I
say I love you I am not
ashamed, nor will anyone
ever ever come close to intimidating
persuading, etc me into thinking
otherwise. I wear you on
my sleeve. I spread you
out wide open with the wing
span of a peacock, yet
all too often with the attention
span of a bullet to the head.
I think its pathetic that the
entire world looks upon a
person with patience and a
calm demeanor as the desired
model citizen. yet theres
something to be said about
the ability to explain

ones self with a toned down,
tune deaf tone. And I will say it: I am what
they call the boy who is
slow. how I metamorphosised
from hyperactive to cement
is for lack of a better knife
to the throat uh, annoying,
aggrevating, confusing
as dense as cement.
cement holds no other
minerals. you can't even find
fools gold in it. its strictly
man made and you've taught
me it's ok to be a man
and in the classic mans world
I parade you around proudly
like the ring on my finger
which holds no mineral.
ALSO          Love Kurt

THE New improved revised
NIRVANA list of Albums
in which the person writing this has
been emotionally affected by. •
inspired to encapsulate what his
thoughts of a lifestyle in which he
MAY be ~~right~~ immersed in for
reasons of looking cool and hip.
OH and by the way maybe to introduce
these elititist obscure, treasures to the
uhabashed

---

**Elo:** Electric light orchestra • The KNACK Get the
~~KNACK~~

(Gold: John ?) 10CC the things we do for love.

HALL and oats. Rich Girl (wild cherry) play that funky music

Leo Sayer ?        Supertramp        EAgles: long run
                   Breakfast in America

Pat Benatar ?      Journey escape.    Reo spedwagen
Fleetwoolmac                          Hi infidility
Rumours            BAY city Rollers ?

Seasons in the sun  Bugles: video      Beatles meet
Terry Jacks         Killed the radio store  the Beatles

I Have been forced to become a reclusive RockStar
IE: No interviews, No radio appearances,                    etc.
    due to the legions of self appointed authorities on music
who are not musicians, who have not contributed anything
artistic to Rock and Roll besides maybe a few second rate
long winded, books on Rock and Roll and most importantly
who are ~~easily~~ the highest group of Mysogynists of all
forms of expression.
I have since the beginning of my first revelation in alternative thought
through the introduction of New Wave - then, Punk rock, then alternate,
soundtracks of Contemporary Classic Rock. Never in years of my awareness
of sexism have I seen a more, radically venemous display of
Sexism in my life ~~than ever before~~ than in the past two
years.   For years Ive observed and watch the a culture
for any hint of sexism and I've found it in relatively small
doses compared to the present state of Rock and Roll.

From Critics darlings to Samantha fox, simply because one of
the members of what used to be thought of as a band with members
Has married an established, ~~see~~ musical success determined by
the establishment of non musical music critics. Something smells fishy!

by this time, All conspiracy theories are very very real with more proof than needed to be bothered with describing. Beaurocracy exists as cancer in the Simplest, most naive, grass roots ~~business~~ businesses of pencil vendors, panhandling, fenzine distribution, home baked hippie cookie sales agents up through the yawn, medical protection, Government related protection agencies, Janitorial positions, and erm, entertainment industries. Journalists will now break their own fingers after engaging in finger prints of exchanging individuals display on their left breast in the form of a o button and they will bow down to let the artists critique themselves and other artists. This is a fanzine written by music fans. we know this to be true because they are musicians. Can they write as well as they play? better.

What about Genres. A heavy metal musician, cannot review, A dance R'n'B soul group. Its that easy.

Elitism = Punk Rock

Capitalism =

253

If you were a music fan than you would contribute to A fanzine.

You have no right to ask the question of: do you have artistic control now that you're signed to a major. for all Journalists are at the mercy of their editors.

Second rate 3rd degree burns.

If we ever win any more awards we will have
3 impersonators come up and accept the awards
3 people who look fairly familiar to us.


VIDeo concept. milk it or scentless apprentice
drunken fucked up me, man in a room full of
people at a party man has gun and is stumbling
around falling down threatening to shoot.
man has wild glossy stare.


Play unplugged soon.


release a compilation tape of favorite punk
Songs with vinyl version of album

♡ Shaped box video

William and I sitting across from one another at a table
(black and white) lots of Blinding Sun from the windows behind us
holding hands staring into eachothers eyes. He gropes me from
behind and falls dead on top of me. medical footage of
sperm flowing through penis. A ghost vapor comes out of
his chest and groin area and enters me Body.

during Solo. Violin shots. Chris as New wave keyboardist.
and very quick edits of strobe light.

image of little 3 year old white arian, blonde girl in K.K.K
outfit being led by the hand of a KKK parent

Same violet colors as in the New order video

Animation Doll footage.     Close up of lillies lyingon lighted
draft Board.    footage of Anatomy models from Kurts collection

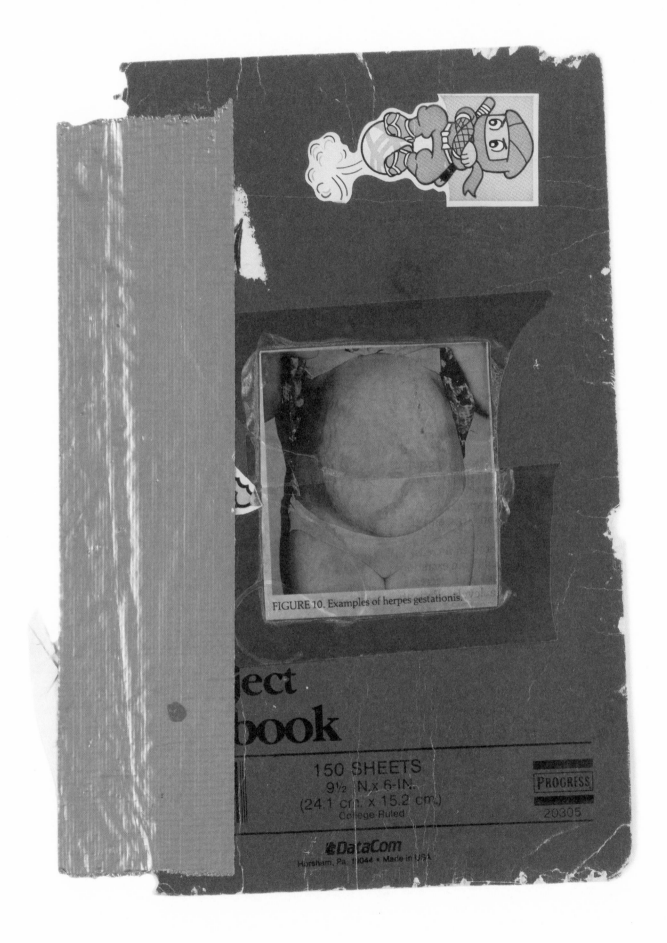

FIGURE 10. Examples of herpes gestationis.

ject
book

150 SHEETS
9½ N.x 6-IN.
(24.1 cm. x 15.2 cm.)
College Ruled

PROGRESS

20305

DataCom
Horsham, Pa. 19044 • Made in USA

# Travelin White Trash Couple
## #1

He Bathes in Gallons of mens Cologne
Hes fillup full of testosterone
She kisses sensually into the lense
They spit their lingo to keep their egos
cleansed.

They keep a lifestyle that is comfortable
they travel far to keep their stomaches full
they have a hairstyle that is out of ~~state~~ date
They seem to claim that their from out of state

---

He keeps his cigarettes close to his heart
She keeps her photographs close to her heart
they keep their bitterness close to their hearts

---

She wants to build herself a windchime house
she does her arts and crafts while staying soused
They probably own about a million cats
they dont care where their from or where their at

They Rip you off and then they leave your town
The local swap meet is their battle ground
She loves him more than he will ever know
He loves her more than she will ever show

**RAW POWER**
**STOOGES**

**SURFER ROSA**
PIXIES

**POD**
BREEDERS

PINK EP
VASELINES

PHILOSOPHY OF THE WORLD
SHAGS

LAND SHARK
FANG

MILLIONS OF DEAD COPS
M.D.C.

1st ep
SCRATCH ACID

1st ep
SACCHARIN TRUST

PEEPEE THE SAILOR
BUTTHOLE SURFERS

MY WAR
BLACK FLAG

ROCK FOR LIGHT
BAD BRAINS

ENTERTAINMENT
GANG OF FOUR

---

**NIRVANA's ATTE off**
**TOP 50**

NEVER MIND BOLLOCKS
SEX PISTOLS

ITS ONLY RIGHT & NATURAL
FROGS

DRY
P.J. HARVEY

DAYDREAM NATION
SONIC YOUTH

GET THE KNACK
THE KNACK

KNOW YOUR PRODUCT
THE SAINTS

ANYTHING BY:
KLEENEX

RAINCOATS LP
RAINCOATS

COLOSSAL YOUTH
YOUNG MARBLE GIANTS

ROCKS
AEROSMITH

WHAT IS IT
EARLY SOCAL. PUNK comp.

GREEN
R.E.M

BURNING FARM cassette
SHONEN KNIFE

TYPICAL GIRLS
SLITS

---

**SOMBRE ROCK**

VOID / FAITH split ep
VOID / FAITH

RITES OF SPRING
RITES OF SPRING

JAMBOREE
BEAT HAPPENING

TALES OF TERROR
TALES OF TERROR

LAST SESSIONS VOL. 1
LEAD BELLY

SUPERFUZZ BIGMUFF
MUDHONEY

YIP JUMP MUSIC
DANIEL JOHNSTON

GENERIC FLIPPER
FLIPPER

MEET THE BEATLES
BEATLES

WE ARE THOSE WHO ACHE WITH AMOROUS LOVE
HALF JAPANESE

LOCUST ABORTION TECHNICIAN
BUTTHOLE SURFERS

for many months I decided to take a break from reading rock magazines mainly to rest and clear my head from all the folk lore and current affair journalism that had been piling up since weve become a lot of peoples (dare I say) breakfast lunch and dinner gossip. Last month I thought I'd take a peek at a few Rock mags to see whats going on and if things have cooled down.

Well, to my estimation many trees have been wasted on account of ~~people~~ bored and boring people who still like to waste space with NIRVANA DRECK. Years ago I knew better than to believe that every article in a news paper reported everything we need to know. as in all the facts man. I knew that newspapers, magazines and history books left out things or embelished based on the special interests of the political and moral beliefs of the share holders or owners of all printed matter. Do you think a History book from the south has basically the same information as on the civil war a history book printed for the northern school districts? Do you think A right wing, Christian owned news paper reports the same as mother Jones magazine? well the rock literary world is a bit more confusing. It's not as cut and dry as the above refferences. People who write for music mags are a collective bunch who are at conflict every day.

As youve heard this cliche many times before music journalists are people who are paid to find as many interesting anectdotes of a musicians personality, and if there isnt enough they must spice it up and if it isnt still spicy enough which is almost always the case then, In steps the editor. an editors job is not to correct grammatical errors. his or her job is to sell magazines and to sell magazines you need to have a cupboard full of spices. So once again a journalist is almost always at the mercy of the editor. ironically journalists are the ones who obsessively try to prove that the musician has no control over their own creativity and ~~the record company~~ is dictated by their record company. and the biggest ~~cliche of~~ and most overly used cliche of the journalist although is too true to ignore is the fact that most journalists have no idea of what its like to write a song, play an instrument or know what it's like to perform on stage in front of people. The choice to become a music journalist is usually after ones realization that they are musically retarded. but theyve worked at tower Records and own a lot of Cd's and rock biographies.

I found at an early age that the same people who share the same truth-witheld due to special interests conspiracy theory are usually the same people who are fans of politically motivated or music that leans towards elements of outspoken truths. PUNK ROCK. for the most part falls under this category. Quite a few years ago I felt that most of these people who listened to punk rock were aware of commercial Rock mag Sensationalism and knew better than to believe what was written in these magazines which have always ignored underground or punk Rock bands because Punk Rock doesnt sell magazines. until now. just like new Wave. punk rock has been cristened a new name by commercial magazines " Alternative music" And just like New Wave only the most commercial bands are featured in these magazines.

The easiest way to advert from the chance of misrepresentation is to use the Question Answer format. it has been proven for years that this is a safe and effective way to report the truth as long as all of the answers are printed in their entirety. When chris said "most Heavy metal kids are dumb" that was printed. What wasn't printed was the rest of it which was," and I was one of those dumb Heavy metal kids. Its not their fault because there are stupid Heavy metal bands carrying on the legacy of sexism and homophobia in white boy rock and roll." The most interesting thing about our supposed contradictory attitudes and statements made almost 2 years ago is that all of those interviews were conducted within a span of 2 to 3 months and anyone given the surprise of becoming instant rock stars against their will have the same thoughts running through their heads. Basically what we felt was a danger. the threat of losing contact with the very people whom we felt shared the same commercial/corporate magazine conspiracy theory as we did. But as it turns out pages and pages of letters bitching about our negative reactions (which were nothing more then precautionary) littered every fanzine this side of the world.

In conclusion those same people who we felt an honest love and mutual bond with bought the current affair hype hook line and sinker. which has left us feeling betrayed. we simply wanted to give those dumb heavy metal kids (the kids who we used to be) an introduction to A different way of thinking and some 15 years worth of emotionally and socially important music and all we got was flack, backstabbing and pearl Jam.

The most strange and admirable discoverie of the three Witches of Warboys, *arraigned, convicted,* and executed at the last Assises at Huntington, for the bewitching of the five daughters of Robert Throckmorton Esquire, and divers other persons, with sundrie Divellish and grievous torments: *And also for the bewitching to death of the Lady Cromwell, the like hath not been heard of in this age.*

LONDON
Printed by the Widdowe Orwin, for Thomas Man, and John Winnington, and are to be solde in Paternoster Rowe, at the signe of the Talbot. 1593.

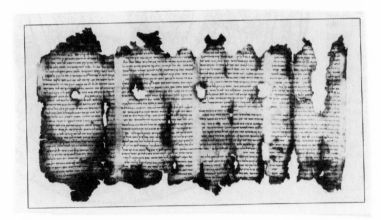

whithin the months between october 1991 thru december 92
I have had 4 four Notebooks filled with two years worth of
Poetry and personal writings and thoughts LYRICS stolen from
me at seperate times. two 90 minute cassettes filled
with new guitar and singing parts for new songs damaged
from a plumbing accident, as well as two of my most
expensive, favorite guitars. I've never been a very prolific
person so when creativity flows, it flows. I find myself
scribbling on little note pads and pieces of loose paper which
results in a very small portion of my writings to ever show
up in true form. Its my fault but the most violating
thing ive felt this year is not the media exxagerations
or the catty gossip, but the rape of my personal
thoughts. ripped out of pages from my stay in hospitals
and aeroplane rides hotel stays etc. I feel compelled
to say fuck you fuck you to those of
you who have absolutely no regard for me as a person.
You have raped one harder than you'll ever know, so again
I say fuck you although this phrase has totally
lost its meaning    FUCK YOU!

        FUCK YOU.

Sore bahrre astray the Govna hs been found dead in a ~~bed~~
He Shouldnt A been bed!

Dead and blasted fed and bearded poet.

~~there is no place for the Republican president candidate in that world~~

90% of the adult American population were not
concerned with nor had any desire to see or heard
about woodstock. 90% of the woodstock Generation are
not old Hippies now with children and the priveledge of
infusing their once young liberal ideals into the new society
in which they now are responsible for

Yes, Every one of our parents likes to hear the same old
NO 1 Hits of the 60's & 70 and lead us to believe that
they were active in the revolutionary methods of thinking
and Idealtic vibrance of nativety they just couldn't wait
to open up and use once they got into power
the majority were then ~~just a~~ a product of fetal inflation
produced by the fear and shock of the world war. ~~and~~
They took the bait, stayed in their classes, remembered
the scriptures of Donna Reid, graduated from high school and
had children. The Hippies are the baby boomers younger
Brothers and sisters and the Hippies were a very small breed
of veal who never managed to teach the basics to theirs
and their older brothers and sisters that of peace, love, restraining
of predsudice of any kind. I remember only one thing about my perception
Hippies when I was a child. by the way my generation is the children of the
older brothers and sisters we who in order of keeping the tradition of rebellion
get Republican tattoos on our asses ~~in spite our natty~~ and dont take a damn thing seriously
to spite our filthy hippie parents. and these sad pattetic sensitive types who cares
the tragic burden of taking everything too serious and making everyone feel uncomfortable
I remember thinking all hippies were evil baby killers like charles Manson.
I only remember a few things about Jimmy Carter, He had big lips
and liked peanuts. I know now that Jimmy Carter was and is a good man
Jimmy Carter is a good, honest, smart man.

Eric Clapton dusty Blues riffs

Hi, I played the snare drum in school band from ~~the fifth~~ grades five to ~~~~ nine. during this time I didn't bother learning how to ~~actually~~ read sheet music, I just ~~waited~~ waited ~~for~~ for the geek in first chair to ~~play~~ learn ~~to play each~~ each song, ~~and~~ then I simply copied him. I ~~got~~ managed

to do well ~~By~~ just fine without ever having ~~to ever learned~~ how to read music. It took me 5 years to realize ~~the~~ ~~How~~ rhythmically retarded ~~I was as a drummer~~, so I sold some of my fathers guns ~~then~~ used the money to purchase my first six string electric guitar. ~~I took one week of lessons~~ I learned everything I needed to know from one week of lessons which ~~are~~ resulted in the famous ~~I learned the~~ musical knowledge of louie louie chords.

E A B

weird Al

I noticed that
~~then~~ I could the ~~you can~~ use finger positions from
the B note anywhere on the guitar, this is
known as the power chord.
~~Then I started writing my~~
And so after figuring out songs like
~~Kingsmen~~ louie louie ~~troggs~~ wild thing, and ~~cars.~~ my best friends girl
I decided that in order to become A big famous
Rock star I would need to ~~start~~ write my
very OWN songs instead of wasting my
time learning other peoples because if you ~~do~~
obstruct ~~study~~ study other peoples music too much It
        Act as A obstruction    IN
may ~~block~~ ~~you~~ developing ~~your~~ your
your very own personal ~~style personal~~ style
        Someone told me that there are                    the
        ~~so~~ Guitar institutes of technology ~~throughout our~~  All across overworld
Greatland.   where they teach you how to be
        A lame un-original jukebox heroe
        with stars in ~~your~~ eyes
                                your

        Uh, Gee I guess what im trying to say
is: theory is A waste of time
Dorian modes are ~~for technically anal~~ Boys with Bad values
make up your own music.
        Eric Clapton plays second rate dusty blues licks.
        Too much practice is like too much sugar.
        weird Al Yankovic is americas modern pop-Rock Genious
        Do your own thing ~~and~~ others ~~the own~~ their own thing.
If you
copy → you'll find yourself in late night
too
much    cocktail-Lounge cover band limbo.
P.S.:   the guitar part is for
        come As you Are is the same As A song cAlled
        the "eighties" by killing joke And
        teen spirit has an uncanny resemblance to Godzilla
                by Blue oyster cult and the culture ACDC

The Guitar has twelve notes
The Guitar is based on mathematics

Guitar oriented ~~rock~~ Rock and Roll has been Around
for over 30 years ~~and~~ when ~~you~~ workin
within the structures of a standard 4/4 Rock ~~time signature~~ ~~rhythm~~
their limitations So ~~think~~ consider this music
Are
book As something just to
own like → A bottle cap collection
or Baseball cards or A family photo album
or an example of just exactly how
not to brighten your musical capabilities—
Happy motoring
love kurt

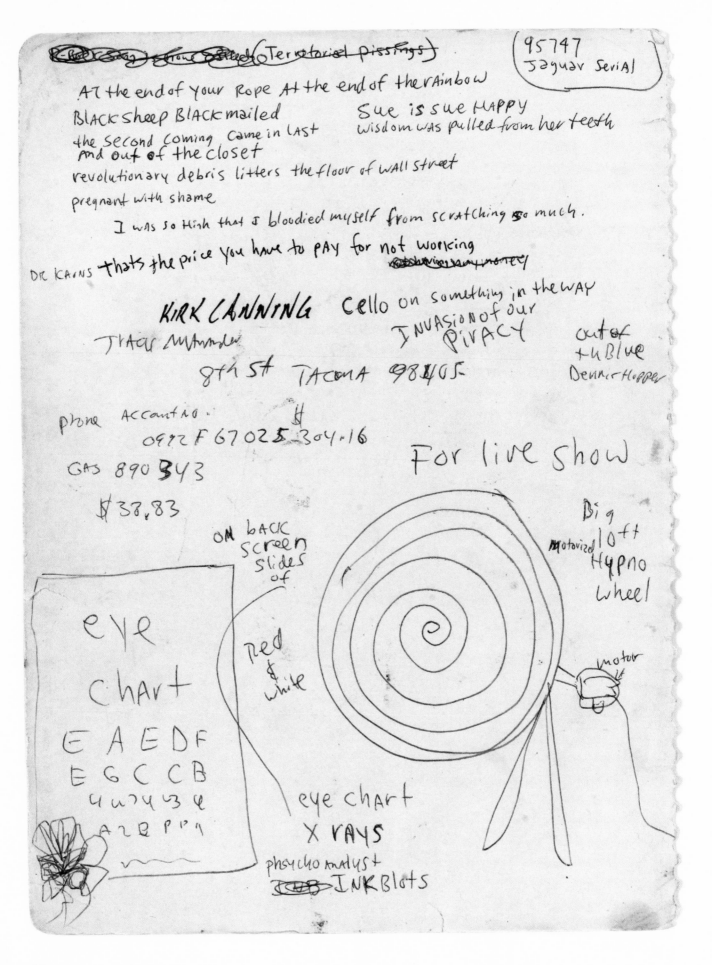

(Territorial pissings)

95747
Jaguar serial

At the end of your Rope At the end of the Rainbow

BLACK sheep BLACK mailed        Sue is sue HAPPY
the Second Coming came in LAST   wisdom was pulled from her teeth
and out of the closet
revolutionary debris litters the floor of WALL street

pregnant with shame

    I was so High that I bloodied myself from scratching so much.

    that's the price you have to PAY for not working
Dr Karns

KIRK CANNING    Cello on something in the WAY
                        INVASION of our
                           PIVACY
Track # Number                                out of
    8th St    TACOMA   98405                  the Blue
                                              Dennis Hopper

phone  Account No.     #
        0992F67025304.16
GAS 890343

$38.83                                For live show

            On bACK
            screen                             Big
            slides                   Motorized 10ft
            of                                 Hypno
eye                                            wheel

                red
chart            &
                white                                  motor
E A E D F
E G C C B
4 ω ɔ Ч 3 ε
A 2 ᙠ P ⁱ ᶯ    eye chart
                X RAYS
              physcho analyst
                    INKBlots

Hope I die before I turn into Pete Townshend.

At this point in our uh, career, before hair loss treatment ~~going~~ and bad credit. ~~I was~~ I've decided that ~~I cant~~ I have no desire to do an interview with Rolling Stone. We couldn't benefit from it because the average Rolling Stone reader is a middle aged ex hippie — turned hippiecrite who embraces the past as "the glory days", ~~and clings to~~ and ~~has~~ a kinder, gentler, more adult approach, towards liberal conservatism. The average Rolling Stone reader ~~is a middle aged youth~~ has always ~~been aware of~~ Denied the underworlds musical options ~~and have denied this~~ unless it becomes an obviously safe ~~as~~ commodity.

I've always felt it was kind of necessary to help out the "now Generation" internally destroy the enemy ~~bay~~ posing as or using the enemy. but the now generation doesn't read Rolling Stone, so we'll jest sit around and wait until the old school starves like dinosaurs while the diaper school begins to litter the floors of wall street with "Real love" – –revolutionary debris. Smells like thirty something.

I would only wear a tie dyed T shirt if it were ~~made from~~ dyed with the urine of phil Collins and the blood of Gerry Garcia.

## Ideas:

Buy a really powerful Ham radio system connected to A satellite dish ~~⊷~~ in order to listen to any college rock station in da country. <u>note</u> House for sale with weeping willow has one in its attic. check into it! per Joan of Landmark realty

# TOP 50 by NIRVANA

Raw power
**Stooges**

Surfer Rosa
**pixies**

POD
**Breeders**

Pink EP
**Vaselines**

Philosophy of the World
**Shaggs**

Land shark
**Fang**

millions of Dead Cops
**M.D.C**

1st EP
**scratch acid**

1st EP
**saccharin Trust**

Pee Pee the Sailor
**Butthole Surfers**

My War
**Black flag**

Rock for light
**Bad Brains**

Entertainment
**Gang of four**

Nevermind the Bollocks
**Sex pistols**

Its only Right and natural
**Frogs**

Dry
**P.J. Harvey**

Daydream Nation
**Sonic Youth**

Get the knack
**the knack**

Know your product
**the Saints**

anything by:
**Kleenex**

Raincoats LP
**Raincoats**

---

Colossal youth
**Young marble Giants**

Rocks
**Aerosmith**

what is this?

Punk comp California
**Green**

**R.E.M**

Burning farm cassette
**Shonen Knife**

typical Girls
**slits**

Combat Rock
**Clash**

Void/Faith EP
**Void/Faith**

Rites of spring
**Rites of spring**

Jamboree
**Beat Happening**

tales of terror
**tales of terror**

last sessions Vol 1
**Leadbelly**

Superfuzz Bigmuff
**mudhoney**

Yip jump music
**Daniel Johnston**

Generic Flipper
**Flipper**

meet the Beatles
**Beatles**

we are those who ache with amorous love
**Half Japanese**

Locust abortion technician
**Butthole Surfers**

Damaged
**Black Flag**

the Record
**Fear**

---

Flowers of Romance
**PIL**

Takes a nation of millions
**Public Enemy**

Beach Party
**marine Girls**

the man who Sold the world
**David Bowie**

Is this real?
**Wipers**

Youth of America
**Wipers**

Over the edge
**Wipers**

Mazzy star
**Mazzy star**

Raping a slave
**swans**

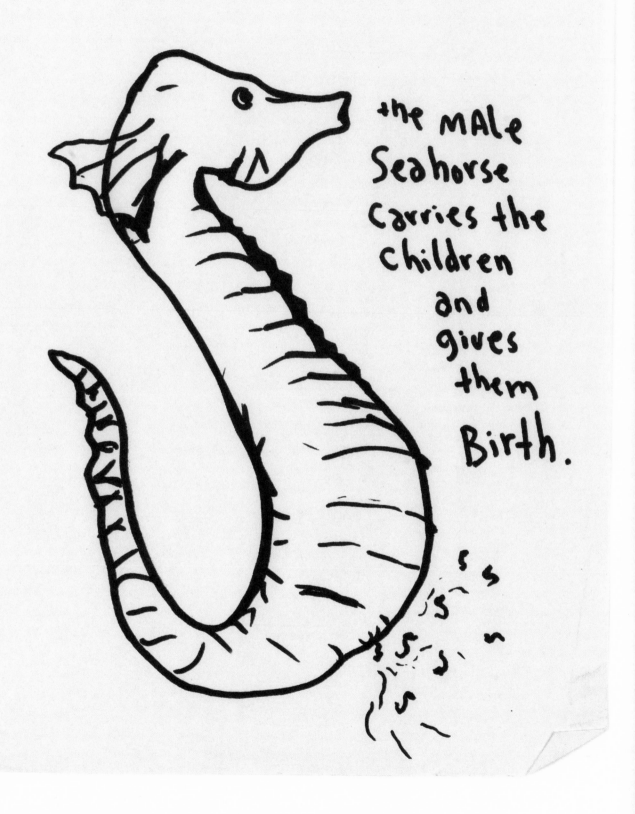

the MAle
Seahorse
carries the
children
and
gives
them
Birth.

when I think of right wing I think of Ronald Reagan clones as mayor in every state of the US.

When I hear the term Right wing I think of Hitler and Satan and Civil war. When I think of Right wingers I think of terrorists ~~and~~ who plot to kill and terrorize the lives of planned parenthood practionists. The reality of actually getting an abortion in this country is very scarce right now due to Randell Terry and his pro life gestapo who gather in churches dressed in the best camouflage ~~possible~~ (~~middle~~ lower-middle-class cameleon polyester from the wrench ies of the home shopping network. IN the house of god, Operation Rescue, (Ter x pet nonprofit organization) plot to unveil yet another helpful household hint to helping their duty as god fearing common folk. They either break into or enter during business hours posing as ~~patients at~~ ~~a~~ abortion clinics and set off            bombs which release a       gas that will absorb into every inch of the clinic ruining every single instrument within that clinic. They put nails in the driveways of clinic staff and doctors. They make never ending threatening and violently abusive phone calls. ~~to clinic staff~~ ~~and doctors~~ They stand outside abortion clinics every day all day with pickets and loud, violent and threatening words of wisdom from GOD. to anyone within miles often ~~at~~ physically stopping patients from entering. Yes these people have criminal records, they have marksman ~~ships~~ and terrorist skills. They are way ahead of the game than their enemy. They steal fetuses from abortion clinic dumpsters and disposal receptices and pass sometimes, hundreds of ~~roast~~ mutilated fetuses between households to be stored in boxes or zip loc baggies in freezers and in the family garage. The ~~fetus~~ rotting deteriorating fetuses are then thrown at senators congressmen or just about anyone involved in government who is a ~~Democrat~~. These people who are terrorists are also people who have basically the same beliefs as white supremists who also claim to act and embrace their ideals on the grounds of GAWD. They post names addresses and phone numbers of patients scheduled to ~~have~~ abortions and the doctors to be performing the operation. They have a computer network of information available everywhere in the united states. Right wing is the foulest, dirtiest, insult a person could be called. These people hate minorities of all color, they will perform mass extermination of everything that is not white, ~~god~~ god fearing and Right wing R is for Republican.

Right now in the state of Florida there are no available abortion doctors or clinics to be serviced by.   Ethnic Cleansing is going on right now in the inner citys of the united states. Blacks, hispanicks and others are being exterminated before they can reach the fifth grade. The Right wing republicans ~~has been~~ are responsible for releasing, crack and Aids in our inner citys. Their logic is ~~better~~ kill living breathing, free thinking humans rather than unknowing unstimulated, growing cells, encased in A lukewarm chamber.

273

Cartoons, Saxophones and Jazz Drumming
do not mix with rock and roll

Cermudgeon

pissy, little
self appointed
Judge-Curmudgeon
Oh the Guilt!
the Guilt!
the autographs
the fame
the lights
the flash
the Glitter
the Guilt
the Guilt

I cant sing
or
play
or
rhyme,
I think thats
just fine

Individual
T shirts

Kurt Don
Cobain

Hair:
whatever
eyes: Closed

Height: smaller
than Chris
weight:
Borderline
anorexic

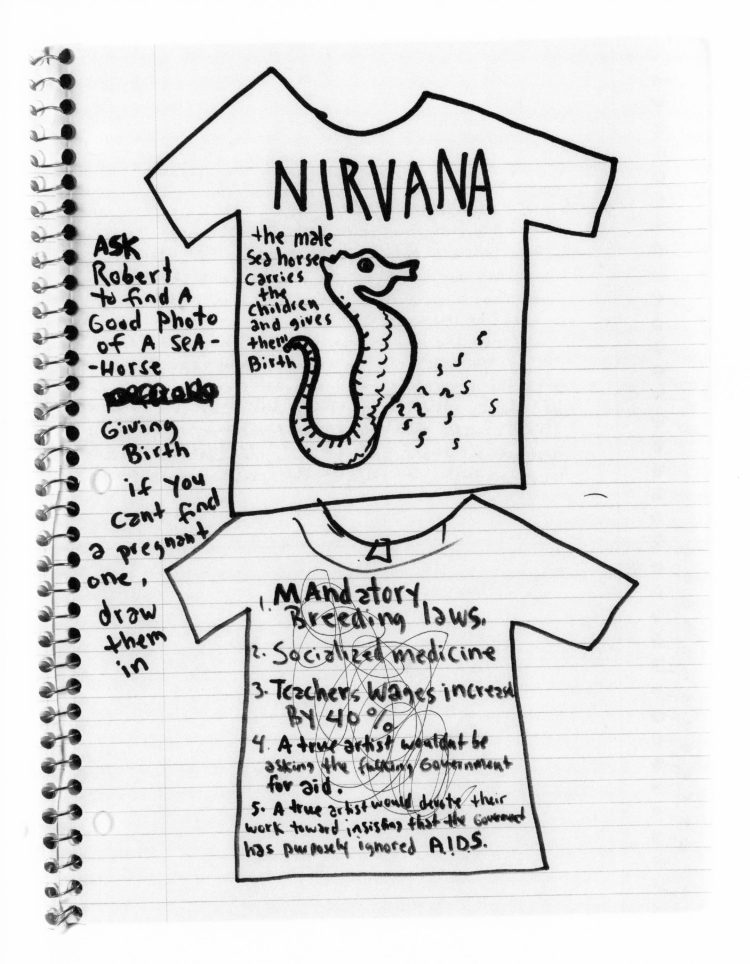

for Boys

step # one: ~~can be mean to girls.~~

remember that your older brothers cousins, uncles, and
your fathers are not your role models. this means
you do not do what they do, you do not do what they say.
They come from a time when their role models told their
sons to be mean to girls, to think of yourself as better
and stronger and smarter than them. They also taught things
like: You will grow up strong if you act tough and
fight the boys who are known as nerds or Geeks,
~~or stick hold letter should pick boys who come from~~
~~families who don't have enough money or the other~~
~~boys who are smarth and get good grades blah blah their dads~~
~~must be sissies if the yet their boys act so smart.~~

~~The early 80's is the acceptance of the counterculture~~

The early 80's saw the white-male-corporate oppressors acceptance ~~it is the~~ of A new musical counterculture stemmed from ~~with~~ the birth of Punk Rock. Well, the clash, the sex pistols and even the melodic accessability of the Ramones didn't break through into the mainstream.

~~Its faith years to~~

~~Its fourteen years later~~

The result of the major labels involvement ended with ex-punk bands ~~is~~ Compromising to such ~~extremes~~ that the only true successes were, gasp! Billy Idol or KAYA 900-900-

Its fourteen years later and they're at it again. So called "Alternative" bands are being signed left and right and the ones with more of an edge towards compromise or mainstream are the ones who will be successful.

NIRVANA will put out a couple of more brilliant albums on their own terms and then become frustrated with being so close to general public acceptance and so ~~in debt~~ financially in debt, that they will eventually result in releasing spineless dance music like Gang of four.

# Rape me

treatment

Black & white film

Hi steve

IN the simplest terms, here it is: . . . .

Go to one or more penitentiarys and shoot ~~film~~ movie film portraits of the most ugly, hardened Criminals available. preferrably bald, big, hairy and ~~tatooed~~. film at least 20 or more of these fine young bucks sitting in their cells and at the visiting booths and tables. from the skinny chest up. we need at least 5 to 10 male Bitches with thick eyeshadow ~~lips~~ and their denim jail shirt sleeves rolledup to ~~and the~~ the bottom half of their shirt tied up exposing thir stomachs

during the lines "my favorite inside sorce ill kiss your open sores appreciate your concern your Gonna stink and burn") we need ~~footage~~ of a Chaotic presscene with lots of reporters with more Cameras and photo flashes ~~on the steps of~~ outside on the steps of a courthouse. then a inside the courtroom a ~~few~~

Rape me treatment     Kurdt

Black and White Portrait-footage of the men
who did the crime and are now doing time.
Big, Bald, sweaty, tattooed love boys cast
from the waist up in their cold, concrete tanks.
lounging on their bunks. striped and branded with
the shadows of prison bars across their chest, face
and walls.    We need about ten to fifteen different
characters. all 200 lbs plus and also about 5 to 8 more
of whom we call the bitches: skinny, feminine,
tight pants wearin, rolled up prison shirts showing
their soft, vulnerable ~~frames.~~ stomaches. 150 lbs and less.
   There are many "Behind Prison Walls," books for
refference.    whites, blacks, Italians.


Close ups of female hands lathering up soap. violent.
scrubbing hands. soapy wash cloth. begging to be clean.
Starting in Black & white fading to color as the hands get cleaner.
Close ups of:
Stock ~~footage~~ of flowers blooming in time lapsed ~~slow~~ motion. } Color
Prefferably lillies, orchids. ya know vaginal flowers.   and now
they wither and shrink up.
Sea horses footage carousing about. floating slowly .
loving life and one another. } Color michael Meisel has found
some of this ~~footage~~ already.

A man lying in a gynecological chair with legs up in sturrops.

Hi fellow Advocatees,

1993 Came and went without notice.

Besides finishing a record in which we are quite proud of, yet getting shit from people claiming "commercial suicide" before it's release. I must say yes, 1993 has been a most fruitful year. Frances is a sprouting, cherubic joy and has helped in more ways than she will ever know.

She has helped us become more relaxed and less concerned with those wacky Right wing ~~conspirators~~ terrorists failed attempts at

Scott

I made about 5 million dollars last year.
And I'm not giving a red cent to that elititist little fuck Calvin Johnson. NO WAY!
I've collaborated with one of my only Idols williamm Burroughs and I couldn't feel cooler.
I moved away to LA for a year and came back to find that 3 of my best friends have become full blown heroine addicts. I've learned to hate Riot Girl. a movement in which I was a witness to its very initial inception because I fucked the girl who put out the first Gurl style fanzine and now she is exploiting the fact that she fucked me. not in a huge way but enough to feel exploited. but thats ok because I chose to let corporate white men exploit me a few years ago and I love it. it feels good. and I'm not gonna donate a single dollar to the fucking needy indie fascist regime. they can starve, let them eat vinyl. every crumb for himself. I'll be able to sell my untalented, very un-genius ass for years based on my cult status.

1993 came and went without realizing it. ~~it happened~~

Besides recording a record in which ~~we~~ are quite proud of
and getting shit ~~for it~~ from people who haven't ~~before anyone~~ heard it
I must say, yes it was a fruitful year. frances is a sproutly
cherubic joy and has helped in more ways then she'll ever know ~~baby~~ by
helping us become more relaxed and less concerned with the foiled
attempts by the right wing conspirators and terrorists to cut off our
rightful supply of fame fortune and the american way God bless this
mess and thank god for the right to choose USA today ~~to love and protect~~ and
uh, kill a queer for God bumper stickers. (thanks william, for the
last remark.) yeah I got to meet and do a record with one of the
only people I admire. that was a plus. and ~~so~~ equally so was
the pleasure of doing the Advocate interview. of all the gut spilling
Ive done Ive never felt so relaxed ~~than~~ with _____

He was very encouraging and sympathetic. what can I say?
thank you I'll always be an Advocate for you fags. I love you.
and apreciate the gracious compliments. ~~for the~~

Hey you should interview Brue la Bruce from canada he's made
some fantastic films. Hope noone felt Ive been too patronizing
~~poster~~   Love kurdt. stay Gay all the way and ~~stay~~ ~~must be defended~~
~~society~~                                        wipe your Ass with USA
                                                                today.


Kevin Allman

Scott

In movies the filmmaker tries to depict true life instances. the most interesting occurances during the subjects time frame are picced out of a span of time. Time is much longer than a movie can show and a viewer will have the patience for. therefore we don't realize how time plays such a gigantic part in the leading up to events. two people may have dinner for 2 hours but only 30 seconds of the most interesting parts of the conversation will be used. I feel time and a persons ability to understand time is very important its the only way I can relate to you the very real way a person becomes addicted to substances If we realize and remember things happen over a period of time. then we may understand how ~~we become a day addict~~ almost everyone who tries hard drugs ie. heroine and cocaine will eventually become literally, a slave to these substances.

I remember someone saying If you try heroine once you'll become hooked. of course I laughed and scoffed at the idea but I now believe this to be very true. not literally, I mean If you do dope once you don't instantly become addicted it usually takes about one month of every day use to physically become addicted. but after the first time your mind say ahh that was very pleasant as long as I dont do it every day I wont have a problem. the problem is it happens over time. lets start with January 1st lets do dope for the first time. conciously you wont do it again for maybe a month. february you'll do it twice. march 3 days in a row. february, 2 days in a row and once more at the end of the month, march, maybe not at all. april 5 days in a row skip 3 once more. may 10 days in a row. during those ten days its very easy to lose track of time it may seem like 3 days but two weeks can go by. The effects are still as pleasant and you can still choose

Hotel Villa Magna, S.A. - Inscrita en el Registro Mercantil de Madrid, Tomo 1993 General, Tomo 1381 de la Sección 3ª. Folio 1. Hoja 10.994 Inscr. 1ª. 26/5/56. CIF A-28-157113

A PARK HYATT HOTEL

PASEO DE LA CASTELLANA, 22 - 28046 MADRID

TELS.: (1) 576 75 00 / (1) 578 20 00  TELEX: 22914 / 27738 VIMA  E TELEFAX: (1) 431 22 86 / (1) 575 31 58

what days you do it so naturally there must not be a problem.
with everyone sometime at least once a year some sort of crisis
happens to everyone, the loss of a friend or mate or relative
this is when the drug tells you to say fuck it.
   every drug addict has said fuck it more times than they
   can count. This example has only taken one page but
   within a year of casual heroine use the person has had
   more days off dope than on. It can slowly and
   gradually consume you because there are 24 hrs in a day
   and no one wants to be hooked. It doesn't happen as
   fast as it does in a movie because a movie quickly
   has to show all the juicy stuff within 2 hrs.
   2 hrs out of 2 years worth of casual drug use is
   nothing. by the time youuve said fuck it the
   long process of trying to stay off begins.
   The first kicke is usually easy if you have pills.
   you basically sleep. which is bad in my opinion
   because you think if its that easy I could get
   hooked and kick for the rest of my life.
   by the second and third time it becomes
   very different. It takes sometimes 5 times
   longer. the psychological factors have set in
   and are as damaging as the physical effects.
   every time you kicke as time goes by it gets
more uncomfortable. even the most needle phobic person can
crave the relief of putting a syringe in their arm. people have
been known to shoot water, booze, mouthwash etc...
drug use is escapism whether you want to admit it or not.
a person may have spent months, years trying to get help. but
the amount of time one spends trying to get help and the years it
takes to become completely drug free is nothing in comparison.
every junkie ive ever met has fought with it at least 5 years and
most end up fighting for about 15 25 years, until finally
they have to resort to becoming a slave to another drug the 12 step
program which is in itself another drug/religion. If it works for
you do it. If your ego is too big start at square one and
go the psychological rehabilit. way. either way youve got
at least 5 to 10 years of battle ahead of you.

## HOTEL EXCELSIOR
### Roma

He said, yes Larry as in Larry King
when we were shooting the film we
found the indigenous people of ALASKA
to be some of the most warm friendly,
blah blah blah etc.. Another retarded
action Adventure side of beef longing to
portray himself as a distinguished actor.
His P.R man transcribed a basic English
101 course on A piece of paper and
Jean Clod Clod Goddammne actor
man must have studied the Answers
to the hallowing questions that Larry
will be asking for at least a week.
Now thats Entertainment! watching
Sylvester Stallone fumble his way through
An interview with that yo duh

Fred Flintstone accent while spewing out sentences that maybe uh A really smart guy might say ya know with a lot of so as well as ' pertaining to, etc. blah.

The indigenous people of ALASKA? what are you fucking talking about? the Eskimos? or the drunken Redneck settlers who never see sunshine who are up to their ball sacks with raw dead fish guts on A boat for 9 months out of the year.

NOTES

A note about the letters: Kurt often wrote a draft before completing the final version of a letter. Some of the letters included in this book represent those drafts, while others are letters that were never sent.

Page 1:
Letter to Dale Crover, the drummer for the Melvins, an Aberdeen rock band that heavily influenced early Nirvana.

Page 15:
Letter to Dave Foster, Nirvana's second drummer, who was fired shortly before the recording sessions for "Love Buzz."

Page 19:
Letter to Mark Lanegan, lead singer of the Seattle band Screaming Trees.

Page 32:
Letter to Jesse Reed, Kurt's best friend from high school.

Page 39:
NIRVANA
Kenichewa
Dear _____.
NIRVANA is a three piece from the outskirts of Seattle WA.
Kurdt-Guitar/Voice and Chris-bass have struggled with too many undedicated drummers for the past 3 years, performing under such names as: Bliss, throat Oyster, Pen Cap Ch[ew] Ted ed Fred etc . . . for the last 9 months we have had the pleasure to take Chad-drums under our wings and develop what we are now and always will be NIRVANA.
3 regularly broadcasted carts on K.C.M.U. (Seattle College Radio also KAOS Olympia)
Played with: Leaving Trains, Whipping Boy, Hells Kitchen, Trecherous Jaywalkers & countless local acts.
Looking for: EP or LP  We have about 15 songs Recorded on 8 Tracks at Reciprocal Studios in Seattle.
Willing to compromise on material (some of this shit is pretty old.)  Tour Any-time forever hopefully the music will speak for itself
Please Reply Thank You  Area Code (206)   N PEAR Olympia WA. 98506

Page 64:
Kurt's questions for a fanzine interview with the Melvins.

Page 252:

I have been forced to become a reclusive Rock Star

IE: No interviews, no radio appearances, etc. due to the legions of self appointed authorities on music who are not musicians, who have not contributed anything artistic to Rock and Roll besides maybe a few second rate long winded, books on Rock and Roll and most importantly who are the highest group of mysogynists in all forms of expression.

I have since the beginning of my first revelation in alternative thought through the introduction of New Wave— then, Punk rock, then alternative soundtracks of Contemporary Classic Rock. Never in years of my awareness of sexism have I seen a more radically venomous display of sexism in my life than in the past two years. for years I've observed and waited like a vulture for any hint of sexism and I've found it in relatively small doses com- pared to the present state of Rock and Roll, from critics darlings to Samantha fox simply because one of the members of what used to be thought of as a band with members Has married an established, musical, success determined by the establishment of non musical music writers. Something smells fishy!

Page 253:

by this time, All conspiracy theories are very very real. With more proof than needed to be bothered with describing. Beaurocracy exists as cancer in the simplest, most naive, grass roots business of pencil vendors, panhandling, fanzine distribution, home baked, hippie cookie sales agents up through the yawn; medical profession, Government related protection agencies, Janitorial positions, and erm, entertainment industries. Journalists will now break their own fingers after engaging in each individuals display of fingerprints on their left breast in the form of a button and they will bow down to let the artists critique themselves and other artists.  This is a fanzine written by music fans. We know this to be true because they are musicians. Can they write as well as they play? better. What about Genres. A heavy metal musician cannot review, a dance RnB soul group. It's that easy.

Elitism = Punk Rock

Capitalism =

Page 254:

If you were a music fan than you would contribute to a fanzine.

You have no right to ask the question: do you have artistic control now that you've signed to a major. for all Journalists are at the mercy of their editors.

Second rate 3rd degree burns

Page 255:

If we ever win any more awards we will have 3 impersonators come up and accept the award  3 people who look fairly familiar to us.

Video Concept. Milk it or scentless apprentice drunken fucked up me, man in a room full of people at a party man has gun and is stumbling around falling down threatening to shoot.

man has wild glossy stare.

play unplugged soon.

release a compilation tape of favorite punk songs with vinyl version of album

Page 256:

❤ Shaped box video

William and I sitting across from one another at a table (Black and White) lots of Blinding Sun from the windows behind us holding hands staring into each others eyes. He gropes me from behind and falls dead on top of me. medical footage of sperm flowing through penis. A ghost vapor comes out of his chest and groin area and enters me Body.

during solo. Violin shots. Chris as New Wave keyboardist and very quick edits of strobe light.

image of little 3 year old white, arian, blonde girl in KKK outfit being led by the hand of a KKK parent

Same violet colors as in the New order video

Animation Doll footage. Close up of lillies lying on lighted draft Board. footage of Anatomy models from Kurts collection

Pages 278-279:

Concepts for "Rape Me" video that was never made.

Page 283-284:

Hotel Villa Magna

Madrid

In movies the filmmaker tries to depict true life instances, the most interesting occurances during the subjects time frame are picked out of a span of time. Time is much longer than a movie can show and a viewer will have the patience for. therefore we don't realize how time plays such a gigantic part in the leading up to events. two people may have dinner for 2 hours but only 30 seconds of the most interesting parts of the conversation will be used. I feel time and a persons ability to understand time is very important. its the only way I can relate to you the very real way a person becomes addicted to substances  If we realize and remember things happen over a period of time, then we may understand how almost everyone who tries hard drugs ie: heroine and cocaine will eventually become literally, a slave to these substances.

I remember someone saying if you try heroine once you'll become hooked. Of course I laughed and scoffed at the idea but I now believe this to be very true. Not literally, I mean if you do dope once you don't instantly become addicted it usually takes about one month of every day use to physically become addicted. but after the first time your mind say ahh that was very pleasant as long as I don't do it every day I won't have a problem. the problem is it happens over time. lets start with January 1st lets do dope for the first time. Conciously you won't do it again for maybe a month. febuary youll do it twice. march 3 days in a row. february, 3 days in a row and once more at the end of the month. march, maybe not at all. april 5 days in a row Skip 3 once more. May 10 days in a row. during those ten days it's very easy to lose track of time it may seem like 3 days but two weeks can go by. The effects are still as pleasant and you can still choose what days you do it so naturally there must not be a problem. with everyone some time at least once a year some sort of crisis happens to everyone, the loss of a friend or mate or relative this is when the drug tells you to say fuck it. every drug addict has said fuck it more times than they can count. This example has only taken one page but within  a year of casual heroine use the person has had more days off dope than on. It can slowly and gradually consume you because there are 24 hrs in a day and no one wants to be hooked. It doesn't happen as fast as it does in a movie because a movie quickly has to show all the juicy stuff within 2 hrs. 2 hrs out of a years worth of casual drug use is nothing. by the time you've said fuck it the long process of trying to stay off begins. The first kick is usually easy if you have pills. You basically sleep. which is bad in my opinion because you think if its that easy I could get hooked and kick for the rest of my life. by the second and third time it becomes very different. It takes sometimes 5 times longer. the psychological factors have set in and are as damaging as the physical effects. every time you kick as time goes by it gets more uncomfortable. even the most needle phobic person can crave the relief of putting a syringe in their arm. people have been known to shoot water, booze, mouthwash etc . . . drug use is escapism whether you want to admit it or not. a person may have spent months, years trying to get help, but the amount of time one spends trying to get help and the years it takes to become completely drug free is nothing in comparison. every junkie i've ever met has fought with it at least 5 years and most end up fighting for about 15 25 years, until finally they have to resort to becoming a slave to another drug the 12 step program which is in itself another drug/religion. If it works for you do it. If your ego is too big start at square one and go the psychological rehabilitative way. either way you've got at least 5 to 10 years of battle ahead of you.


Page 285-286:

Hotel Excelsior

Roma

He said, yes Larry as in Larry King when we were shooting the film we found the indigenous people of Alaska to be some of the most warm friendly, blah blah blah etc. Another retarded action adventure side of beef longing to portray himself as a distinguished actor. His P.R. man transcribed a basic English 101 course on a piece of paper and Jean Clod goddammne actor man must have studied the Answers to the hallowing questions that Larry will be asking for at least a week. Now thats Entertainment: watching Sylvester Stallone fumble his way through an interview with that yo duh Fred Flintstone accent while spewing out sentences that may be uh a really smart guy might say ya know with a lot of as well as, pertaining to, etc. blah. The indigenous people of Alaska? What are you fucking talking about? the Eskimos? or the drunken Redneck settlers who never see sunshine who are up to their ball sacks with raw dead fish guts on a boat for 9 months out of the year.